JUAREZ
Hero of Mexico

JUAREZ
Hero of Mexico

Nina Brown Baker

Adapted by
WILLIAM KOTTMEYER
St. Louis Public Schools

Illustrated by
STEPHEN S. BLOOMER

WEBSTER DIVISION, McGRAW-HILL BOOK COMPANY
St. Louis • New York • San Francisco • Dallas • Toronto • London • Sydney

The Webster Everyreaders

The EVERYREADERS were selected from the great literature of the world and adapted to the needs of today's children. This series retains the flavor of the originals, providing mature content and dramatic plot structure, along with eye appeal designed to motivate reading.

This approach was first developed in the renowned St. Louis Reading Clinic by Dr. Kottmeyer and is the direct outgrowth of wide and successful teaching of remedial reading.

A high interest level plus the carefully controlled vocabulary and sentence structure enable pupils to read the stories easily, confidently, and with enjoyment.

Adapted from *Juarez, Hero of Mexico* by Nina Brown Baker, by permission of the *Vanguard Press,* Inc., Copyright, 1942, by Nina Brown Baker.

CONTENTS

CHAPTER 1. THE SHEPHERD BOY

A little Indian boy sat looking into a mountain pool. He rubbed his thin little stomach. Poor little Benito was hungry. Since Grandma died, he had never had enough to eat.

Uncle Bernardino gave out the food. Big people got a lot. Little people got only a little. Benito was twelve now, but he was very small. A little bowl of bean soup—that was enough, said Uncle Bernardino.

Uncle Bernardino was different. He had a great, fat stomach. He ate lots of corn cakes. He got the meat. His soup bowl was big. That was right and fair, said Uncle Bernardino. Little orphan boys had nothing to say.

Benito did not try to. When he had been three, his father and mother died. Then he had gone to Grandma's house. It was not bad while Grandma lived. Even Josefa, his older sister, did not mind Uncle Bernardino then. But then Grandma died. Uncle Bernardino got worse and worse. At last Josefa had enough. Josefa ran away.

"Hi, Benito!"

Through the corn field came Apolonio, the horse

trader's son. Apolonio was fifteen. He was a big boy. His arms were full of green corn.

"Get some sticks for a fire," he said. "Look! I've got enough for both of us. We'll have a feast."

"But Polonio—did you steal them? What will Don Estévan say? It's his corn field."

"Oh, he won't care." Apolonio threw the corn down. "Besides, he won't know. He's down at the inn drinking. Get busy now, if you want some. Bring some stones, too. We'll build a good fire. Hurry, now, if you want to eat."

Benito did want to eat. He had eaten one corn cake that morning. He got one corn cake when he took the sheep out every morning. Benito was feeling empty.

He did what the big boy told him. He brought back two large stones. Benito built the fire. Apolonio made some mud and packed it around the corn. Then he put the corn into the fire. When the mud was hard, the corn would be baked just right. While they waited, Benito talked.

"Before you came, Polonio, some mule drivers stopped. They had come down from the city. They had wonderful news. I could hardly believe it. I asked them about my sister, Josefa—"

"You little fool!" said Apolonio. "Your uncle sends you to watch the sheep. What do you do? Play around the road, bothering everybody. Your sister! She ran away two years ago. You have never heard from her. You don't even know if she got to the city. What if she did? The city is Oaxaca—it's big. There are thousands of people. How could anybody find one poor Indian girl? She wasn't even pretty!"

"No," said Benito, "she wasn't. But Josefa is good. I love her dearly, Polonio. But let me tell you! They *did* see her. These mule drivers did see her—at the market place. Juan saw her and spoke to her. He says she is happy and gets enough to eat. Enough to eat! Think of that!"

"Well, that's a change after living in your uncle's house. But maybe it isn't true, Benito. I know Juan. He's a liar. I'll bet he just made up the story to shut you up."

"Oh, no, Polonio! He did see her. He talked to her. She's working for a rich family. She had a boy with her. He carried two baskets. My sister buys the food for a rich family. That shows she has risen in the world."

"Ha! Such a story!" cried Apolonio. "But if it were true, what good would it do you? She'll forget you."

"Not Josefa!" cried Benito. "She asked for me. Juan said so. She wished I was with her. I wish it, too. If only—"

The two boys had their backs to the road. As they

talked, they turned the corn. They did not see the angry farmer coming. Suddenly Don Estévan grabbed them.

"So!" he growled. "I see smoke rising from my field. I think my field is burning. I hurry. What do I find? Two boys roasting corn! Whose corn? Mine. Which one stole my corn?"

"I—I—," began Benito. Then Apolonio said:

"Oh, isn't that too bad! I was just walking by. Little Benito asked if I wanted some corn. I didn't ask how he had gotten it. I thought his uncle gave it to him. If he stole it—"

"*If!*" cried Don Estévan. "Look!" He pointed to his field. The stalks were broken. He reached out and grabbed Benito's ear.

"We'll go see your uncle, little thief. Let's see what he has to say."

Benito swallowed hard. "Don Estévan," he said, "I did not steal them. I will tell you the truth. It was not I."

"Little Juarez (wär′ as) lies, too," said Apolonio.

"Yes," said Don Estévan. "He is no good. Well, his uncle will take care of him. Come on, you!" He jerked poor Benito's ear again.

"I'll bring his sheep," said Apolonio. "Don Bernardino would not want them to run loose. I'll bring them home."

4

"You are a good boy, Apolonio." Don Estévan dragged Benito after him.

It was already late afternoon. Uncle Bernardino still lay in his hammock. The grape vines made cool shade. Uncle Bernardino had no wife, so he rested most of the day.

He sat up as Don Estévan came with Benito. The farmer told his story. Uncle Bernardino's face got an angry red.

"Talk up, boy," he said angrily. "So you are a thief! You bring shame to my house. Why did you do it?"

Benito raised his eyes. "I am no thief, Uncle. I did not take the corn."

"Listen to him!" cried Don Estévan. "He is a thief and a liar. Who stole the corn if you did not?"

Benito said nothing. What was the use? Polonio had said he had not taken the corn. Polonio was the horse trader's son. The men believed him. They would never believe Benito.

Uncle Bernardino reached for his whip. He used it on horses. He patted the whip. Benito shivered.

Apolonio came then. He held the roasted corn in his arms. He bowed and held the ears out to Don Estévan.

"Your wife will not have to cook your supper, sir," he said. "They are yours, so I brought them."

5

"You are a good boy, Polonio," said the farmer.

"Thank you, sir." Apolonio turned to Uncle Bernardino. "I drove your sheep into the yard. Benito did not bring them in. I gave them a drink, so you need not worry about them. I am glad to help my father's friends."

"That was good, my boy. Did you count them? There should be twelve."

"Oh, no, sir—eleven," said Apolonio.

"Eleven? But there were twelve! Twelve fat sheep Benito drove off this morning. He has lost one, then. I'll see about that."

Don Bernardino got up to look. Don Estévan and Apolonio followed. Benito stood where he was.

The three were soon back. Uncle Bernardino was boiling. He held his whip, but did not use it. He began to shout and scream at the boy. Apolonio spoke up again.

"I am sure I did not miss any sheep," he said. "There were only eleven. I brought them all. But if one is missing—"

"Well?"

"Why, sir, Benito told me he had talked with Juan and the mule drivers. Here's my guess. Juan talked to Benito while the others stole the sheep. My father says Juan is a thief."

"It could be," said Don Estévan. "If the boy was

playing around the road instead of watching his sheep—"

"This is too much!" shouted Uncle Bernardino. He stepped forward and raised the whip.

Then his hand fell. "Later," he said. "I'll see you later. First you have work to do. You go after the mule drivers. You get that sheep back. And listen to this. *Don't come back without that sheep!*"

Benito stood again beside the pool. The sun was going down. It was cold. He poked at the dying fire he had built earlier. He was hungry, but not one ear of corn was left. The clay showed that Apolonio had eaten some before he brought the rest back.

Benito looked around for the sheep. He saw none. Then he went back to the road and stood there.

"I guess the mule drivers did get it," he said. He did not know them, except Juan. They had left five hours ago. They would now be many miles away. How could he hope to catch them?

And what if he could? He could not make them give the sheep back. They were grown men. They carried guns and knives. What could a little boy do? Juan would not help him. Benito remembered that Juan had once been caught stealing chickens. If he would steal a chicken, why not a sheep?

Could Juan have lied about his sister? Benito tried

to remember the whole story. If it was a lie, it was a good one. Juan had even told him for whom Josefa worked. It was an Italian family. What had he said? *Maza*. That was it. The family was named Maza.

The sun was almost down now. A cold wind sprang up. Benito shivered again. A pair of short cotton pants and a coat of palm leaves were his only clothes.

He looked down at the road. He must walk miles and miles. He must find a gang of armed men. He must bring back the stolen sheep—or face Uncle Bernardino.

He looked the other way. That way lay Oaxaca. Maybe Josefa was there. Maybe not.

What should a little twelve-year-old boy do? He had no friends. He was all alone. He was cold and hungry.

Young Benito Juarez started marching up the road—to the city. Benito had made up his mind. He was running away from home.

"If you please—"

The light was dim in the Maza kitchen. The young cook stirred a great pot of soup. She looked up. Somebody was standing at the door.

"No beggars here," she said. "Go away, boy."

But the little boy knew the cook's voice.

"Josefa!" he cried. "My sister!" He threw himself into her arms.

"Benito, my little one," said Josefa. "I can't believe it's really you. So Juan did see you, then? I told him to find you. I was afraid he would not do it."

"He is a bad man, I think," said Benito. "He must have stolen Uncle's sheep. But I'm not angry. He told me where you were."

"Sheep? What's this about a sheep?" asked Josefa.

Benito told her the story. Her eyes flashed. She held her brother close.

"You shall not go back to him," she cried. "You have seen the last of Uncle Bernardino. But tell me, Benito, how did you ever get here? How did you find me?"

"Why, Josefa, I walked. See?" He held out his

bare brown feet. They were bleeding and caked with dust. "I walked three days," he said. "I did not sleep much. I was afraid Uncle might catch me. I did not want to go back."

"What did you eat?"

"Oh, some berries. Sometimes I found some. I drank water. It fills you up when you are hungry."

"How did you find me?"

"I went to the market place. There I asked for Señor Maza's house. I remembered what Juan told me. At first nobody could understand me. They talk a strange language here."

"It's Spanish," said Josefa. "Everybody speaks Spanish here. You will have to learn it. It's not hard. I can speak it well."

"At last I found an Indian like us. He told me how to get here. So here I am. Will you let me stay, Josefa? I can't go back to Uncle. I'd rather die."

"You shall not go back," said Josefa. "We'll see what we can do. First, let's fill your empty stomach. Go wash yourself."

Benito sat on the floor. He held the bowl between his knees. He ate as the Indians ate. He fished out the meat with his fingers. The soup he drank by raising the bowl to his mouth.

Josefa sat beside him, working. She patted out flat corn cakes—*tortillas*. She talked as she worked.

"Just think, Benito. I am cook here. Me — the cook!"

"Why not?" said Benito. "You must be the best cook in the world, Josefa. You make wonderful soup. These people are good to you, then?"

"Señora Maza is an angel," said Josefa. "She even looks like an angel. She has beautiful red hair. And she is kind, Benito! Her voice makes music when she talks."

"And the Señor Maza? How is he?"

"Oh, he is a fine man. Always he laughs and makes jokes. He is good to everybody. All the servants love him. Do you know why I am alone today? It is a feast day—a *fiesta*. He let all the servants go. That's how kind he is."

Benito listened eagerly. This was not like Uncle Bernardino's house. Suddenly the door opened. Little Master José Maza came running in.

"Josefa," he called, "company for dinner. Father's friend, Father Antonio, is coming. Say—who is this boy?"

Benito jumped up. The Maza boy was five years old. His skin was light. His hair was red. He wore Mexican clothes—a black velvet suit and a lace collar.

"What is your name, boy?" he said in Spanish.

Benito looked at Josefa. He didn't understand.

12

"He asks your name, Benito," said Josefa. Josefa turned to José. "My brother knows no Spanish, little master. He speaks Indian."

"Oh! He is your brother, Josefa? Will he stay here?"

"I hope so, little master. I love him very much. He would work hard and asks no pay. But that is for your father to say."

"Papa will say yes—if you wish it," said José. "I like you, Josefa. You make me cookies and sing me Indian songs. I will ask papa to let him stay."

He smiled at Benito. "Eat, boy," he said. "This is your home."

Little José did not forget to ask his father. That night Señor Maza sent for Benito. Señor Maza could not speak Indian, but Father Antonio could. Benito told him his story.

"And you have never been to school?" asked Father Antonio.

"Never. I can not read or write or speak Spanish."

"You have no Spanish blood, then?"

The boy threw back his head proudly. "I have not, sir. I am no half-breed—no *mestizo*. Me, I am all Indian."

Father Antonio smiled. "I like this boy," he said. "Too many Indians say they have white blood."

He turned to Benito again. "You are not sorry you are an Indian, then? Are you proud of it?"

Benito's eyes flashed. "Yes, I am. We were a great people once. Maybe we will be again."

"Well, Father Antonio, what do you say?" asked Señor Maza. "Shall I keep him?"

"He is a strange boy," said Father Antonio slowly. "But I like him, Maza. I like him. Take him. He will work hard."

Señor Maza smiled. "Then tell him he may stay. I will feed him and give him a bed. He gets no pay. Let him help his sister."

Benito let out a deep breath. It was wonderful to have a home—and a full stomach.

CHAPTER 3. BENITO BECOMES A STUDENT

Señor Maza could easily take another kitchen boy. He already had six or seven. They ate in the kitchen and slept in the stable. They helped the other servants. One more made no difference.

But to Benito it made all the difference in the world. For the first time he had enough to eat. And that was not all. He had a warm place to sleep. He got kind words instead of blows.

14

Benito quickly picked up Spanish. Soon he could do what was asked of him. He worked hard and willingly. After six months Señor Maza called for him.

"You have been a good, hard-working boy," he said. "I want you to stay as long as you want. But something has come up. You remember Father Antonio?"

"I do, Señor."

"He needs a boy in his house. He likes you. He wants me to send you to him. What do you say?"

"Sir," said Benito, "he is a kind man. You, too, are a good, kind man. I am glad to work for you. I'll be glad to work for him if you wish."

And so Benito Juarez started another new life. Father Antonio was not a church priest. He lived in his own house. He took care of the priests' library books.

Father Antonio did more than mend the books. He was a man of much learning. He knew and loved the books he worked on. Soon Benito learned to love the books, too.

Benito was a good servant. He kept the little house clean. Every day he cooked the meals. The rest of the time he patched and mended the books. The old priest was glad to see Benito grow to love them.

The books did not make very exciting reading.

But Benito knew the print was *words*. Learning to read was not easy for him. Day after day he worked away at it. He learned to write, too. Many of the older books were hand written. They had to be copied over. It was a proud day when Benito copied a page in a clear hand.

It was a proud day for Father Antonio, too. He was so happy he boasted to his friends. Most of them shook their heads. How could an Indian learn from books? Everybody knew only whites could learn from books.

Father Antonio did not believe that. He knew the first Spanish explorers had not believed it, either. Their priests had taught the Indians. They had built the first college in North America to do it. But that was long ago. As more white men came, they crowded the Indians out of the schools. "The Indians can learn," said Father Antonio. "They just don't get a chance."

It was an evening in October, 1821. Benito had now been three years with Father Antonio.

"Make some little honey cakes tonight, Benito," said Father Antonio. "We shall have company for supper. Can you guess who?"

Benito smiled. "Master José?" he asked. "I am glad. I do not see him very often. When I see Josefa, his teacher is with him."

"Yes, Señor Maza wants him to go to the priests' college. I don't think he wants to go."

"Is Señor Maza coming, too?"

"Yes. When we have eaten, take Master José home. I want to talk to Señor Maza alone."

Benito took the boy home.

"I don't like my teacher," said Master José. "He wants me to learn to spell. Why should I learn to spell? I'm going to be an artist when I grow up. I'm going to paint pictures of great battles. Say, can you spell, Benito? Don't you think it's foolish?"

"No, I like spelling, Master José. In spelling, a word is right or wrong. You can *know* if a word is right. I like *right* things."

"Say, Benito, papa says I'm to go to the Santa Cruz College when I'm twelve. I don't want to. I want to learn to paint."

"But there is no other college here, Master José. All gentlemen's sons go there. You must go, too."

"Maybe. Maybe not. Papa could send me to Paris. Some schools there teach nothing but painting. No reading, no Latin, no spelling. That's the school for me."

Benito laughed. He waved to Josefa, who was waiting for them. He stayed to talk to her a few minutes after José had gone in.

"Is Señor Maza with Father Antonio now?" she said.

"Why, yes. They had something to talk about. That's why I brought José home."

"Ah, yes. I've heard about that. But I may not say anything."

"What do you mean, Josefa? What is this secret?"

"I can't tell you," she said. There was a tear in Josefa's eye. "They are the best people in the world, these Mazas! Oh, Benito, you are a lucky boy. You must pray for them."

"I do, Josefa. I pray for Father Antonio, too. He has been as a father to me. Well, if you won't tell your secret, I'll go back. I have to do some studying."

"You and your books!" said Josefa, smiling. "Get home, then. But I don't think you will study much tonight."

Benito would have gone quietly to his little room. As he passed, Father Antonio called him. "Come here, Benito. We have something to say to you."

"Yes, sir."

He went in and waited. Señor Maza laid down his cigar.

"Come closer, boy. Father Antonio has something to tell you."

Benito looked at Father Antonio. The old man smiled kindly at him.

"Benito, we are talking about you," he said. "How would you like to go to the Santa Cruz College?"

"I, sir? I don't understand."

"Then you shall. Benito, you have learned well here with me. You have brains. We should not make a servant of you. I think you can be a man of learning. Señor Maza thinks so, too."

Señor Maza nodded. "I am no book man myself. But I believe Father Antonio. I'm willing to back you."

"See, Benito?" The old priest was excited. "Do you see what that means? Señor Maza will pay your way. On Monday I will take you there."

Benito could not answer. Santa Cruz! He had seen the rich young men going there. They wore long black gowns and carried books. Benito had never even been jealous. He never thought he had a chance to go to school. Now he could learn!

"Well, boy?" said Señor Maza. "Speak up. What do you say?"

"Sirs, I do not know what to say. I am very, very thankful. But—"

"Say no more. You show them that an Indian can learn, too."

"Yes, sir. You shall never be ashamed of me."

"We know that. Come, let's drink to Benito, our student."

19

They filled three wine glasses. Old Father Antonio put his hand on Benito's shoulder.

"Here's to Benito Juarez," he said. "Benito Juarez, the Indian student!"

CHAPTER 4. SCHOOL DAYS

So, at fifteen, Benito went to school for the first time. Santa Cruz was an old-fashioned school. The boys were not asked to think for themselves. What they learned was in books. If you could remember, you were a good student.

Some boys carried their books home and studied. They got high marks. Others studied just enough so they would not fail. They had a good time.

Most of the boys lived in town. They were white, and proud of it. The ones who had Indian blood tried to hide it. The *mestizos*—who had Indian blood —were ashamed because they were not all white.

Benito Juarez was the only full-blooded Indian there. He learned a bitter lesson the first week he was there. The other boys and the teachers did not like Indians. They thought no Indian should go to school. They thought they were better than he.

Benito said nothing to Father Antonio or Señor

Maza about this. He did not tell that the others laughed and sneered at him. He went his way quietly, studying as hard as he could.

He had always been a smiling, friendly boy. But no young Mexican wanted to make friends with an Indian. Every afternoon the boys poured out into the streets. By twos and threes they walked home together, talking and laughing. But always one boy walked alone—Benito.

He wore an old patched black gown. Father Antonio had begged it from a priest. It was so long, Benito often stumbled over it. Then the other boys had a good laugh at the poor Indian lad.

Benito became more of an Indian than ever before. When he spoke, he said little. When he was happy, he never showed it. If he was sad, he did not show that, either.

CHAPTER 5. BENITO MAKES A FRIEND

But at last, in his fifth year at school, Benito found a good friend. Miguel Méndez was a lawyer's son. He was a thin, sickly, crippled boy. Because of his bad health he had never been to school. He had taught himself by reading his father's books.

His head was full of what he had read. His father had many books about science. Miguel was more interested in science than in religion. At Santa Cruz the boys studied religion. Schools in those days taught very little science.

Miguel talked about the science books in his classes. But not for long. The teachers quickly stopped him. But Miguel had to talk to somebody. He picked the quiet Indian, Benito Juarez. He lent him books. He walked home with him, talking always about science. Benito read the books and listened to his new friend. A new world opened for him.

Miguel's father and others were getting more interested in science. These men were talking about a new school for their boys. They wanted a school which would teach science.

Mexico became free from Spain in 1821. In that year Benito had started school. In 1824 Mexico got its constitution. The constitution said the government would pay for the schools. And so, in 1826, a school of Arts and Sciences opened in Oaxaca.

A priest, Father Aparicio, became head of the new school. He was known for his kindness and great learning. Miguel was one of the first students. He would not rest until he got Benito to go. Benito was eager to start. He took Miguel home to talk to

Father Antonio. They called Señor Maza in. Benito explained. He had not finished at Santa Cruz, but he wanted to change schools.

Señor Maza was on the boys' side. "I'm for the new school," he said. "I've heard all about it. My boy José wants to go. He thinks he can learn to paint there."

"But what is this school all about?" asked Father Antonio. "Do you want to be a painter, Benito? Who put that idea into your head?"

Benito turned to the old man. Father Antonio was getting old. His eyes were dim. He could not hear well any more. Benito spoke clearly and slowly.

"No, sir," he said. "Master José wants to be a painter. I want to go to the new school, though. I want to learn some science."

"New school? Is the old school not good enough?"

Benito looked at Señor Maza.

"The new school is better," said Maza. He shouted in Father Antonio's ear. "Everybody says so. Father Aparicio has the school."

"Ah, a fine man, a fine man. I know him well. Will they teach Benito to be a priest there?"

Maza and Benito did not know what to say. They knew Father Antonio had always hoped Benito would be a priest. Benito looked at the poor old man. He laid his hand on his shoulder.

"Father," he said, "I'll do as you say. Say so and I'll forget about the new school."

"But tell me what you really want, Benito. Do you not want to be a priest?"

"I want to please you, Father. It is for you to say."

"Well—well, I don't know. You have not lost your faith?"

"Oh, no, sir! That could never happen. Whatever I do, do not be afraid of that."

The old man leaned forward. He looked at Benito's face. At last he spoke. "Then let it be as you ask, lad."

And so Benito Juarez went to the new school. The classes were small. You would laugh at the science rooms today. But the boys were all eager to learn. Father Aparicio was a great teacher.

He was glad to have Indian students. Many Indian boys came to the new school. They did not have to pay. For the first time, many Indian boys had a chance to learn.

Father Aparicio liked Benito. He lent the young Indian books he could get nowhere else. He helped him after classes. At the end of two years Father Aparicio asked him to teach at the school. Benito helped the Indian students, especially.

Benito did not stop studying. Now he began to

study law. Soon he liked the law as well as science. When Benito Juarez said, "It is the law," he meant that the law must be obeyed.

CHAPTER 6. A LITTLE MEXICAN HISTORY

Benito Juarez was born March 21, 1806. Mexico was then Spain's colony. Spain owned Central America, too, and most of South America. The United States was the only republic in America.

Columbus had found America for Spain. Then many Spanish explorers had come to hold the land. Cortez had taken Mexico. Pizarro had won Peru.

The Spaniards held America for three hundred years. But the Spanish colonists saw what the United States had done. They knew the French had freed themselves from bad kings. They wanted freedom also. Bolívar was fighting against Spain in Venezuela. San Martín was leading the people in Argentina. Mexican leaders, too, were saying their country should be free.

In 1821 Mexico finally freed herself from Spain. Benito Juarez was then fifteen years old. During the next few years the Mexicans tried to set up a free government. They had a hard time.

Our own people had a better start. We had long had town meetings. We had something to say, even when the English ruled us. We knew how the English government worked.

The white Mexicans had never had anything to say while Spain ruled. The Mexican Indians had nothing to say. The Spanish governor ruled and the Spanish army made everybody obey.

Most Mexicans were Indians or part Indian. Our own country had white men who knew government. Our Indians had no part in the government. But in Mexico many leaders were Indians. For three hundred years they had been badly treated. Now they wanted a voice in the government.

Then there were the rich land owners. They did not like Spanish rule either. These rich men liked the *way* the Spaniards ruled. They wanted a few rich men to rule the country. They did not care to help the poor Indians. Many of them had seen the king's court at Madrid. Now they wanted to have their own king.

The younger, bolder men, especially the Indians, wanted to forget about Spain. They wanted a free country like the United States. These men called themselves the "liberals." The rich land owners called themselves the "conservatives."

There were many whites among the liberals.

The doctors, lawyers, and others were often liberals. Most Indians were liberals. The half-whites—the mestizos—were with the conservatives. They usually worked for the rich land owners and were on their side.

The conservatives were stronger. They met and decided to get a European prince to rule them. They even tried to get a Spanish prince. But Spain said she wanted nothing to do with rebels.

Other princes were not interested either. They wanted to stay in Europe. They did not want to come to a strange, wild land so far away.

The conservatives talked for three months. But then the army settled the question themselves. A rich young man, Don Agustín Iturbide, had fought well against Spain. The soldiers decided he would make a good ruler. So they just said, "Here is our new ruler." The conservatives agreed. They called him Agustín I. For the first time since Montezuma, Mexico had a Mexican ruler.

Agustín ruled less than a year. Then congress asked him to leave.

In 1823 a new congress met. Those who wanted a republic won out this time. President Monroe of the United States had just warned Europe's rulers that America was for Americans. The princes wanted to come less now than ever before.

The congress finally decided to have a republic like ours. They wrote a constitution much like ours. In 1824 they held their first president's election. An Indian, General Victoria, was the first president.

President Victoria had a hard time staying his four years. The next fifty years were times of trouble and bitter revolutions. Always the liberals and the conservatives fought each other. The liberals wanted a better life for the poor man. The conservatives fought to keep what they had.

There was another reason for the trouble. Many Mexican leaders were interested only in themselves. They often jumped from the side of the rich to the side of the poor and back again. When they saw a chance to get power or money, they did.

One of these leaders was Santa Anna. He was a soldier, a great talker, and an actor. He knew how to make a hero out of himself. Sometimes everybody was for him. At other times the people got tired of him. Several times he had to leave the country. But always he came back, got the people on his side again, and got into office once more. This went on for thirty years.

Benito Juarez made many enemies during his life. Santa Anna was the worst. Santa Anna hated him bitterly. The two men first met in the Oaxaca streets in 1828.

CHAPTER 7. THE MEXICAN NAPOLEON

Benito Juarez and his friend Miguel had gone to church. They stopped on the church steps.

"Want to take a walk?" asked Miguel. "We have been too busy with our books. Things have been happening in Oaxaca. Let's try to get a look at Santa Anna. He's in town, you know."

"I don't want to see him," said Benito. But he walked with his friend. "Santa Anna is a rebel, nothing more."

"Oh, come now, Benito," laughed Miguel. "You and I voted for the liberal man, Guerrero. We hoped he would be president. You did not like it when the votes showed Pedraza had won. You even think Pedraza cheated. Now, why blame Santa Anna? He is just trying to get Guerrero in."

"Because he is trying to do it by force. That is not the right way," said Benito. The two moved slowly down the street.

"Yes," said Benito, "I know it's hard to do right. I was for Guerrero, as you say. He is half Indian and a liberal. He should be president. Pedraza is a rich man. He would do nothing for the poor people.

29

I am sorry he was elected, Miguel. But—he was *elected*. They cheated, I guess. But let's count the votes again. Let's hold another election. We must do what the law says. We cannot do it with guns."

Before Miguel could answer, they heard somebody shouting. A carriage came rattling down the street, going fast. The old man inside looked angry.

"What in the world has happened?" Miguel jumped back. Another carriage rattled by, then another. They were rich people and they all looked angry. A mob of men now came on foot. They were shouting and laughing.

"Santa Anna's men, I think," said Miguel. "I wonder what they have been up to. Did you see their clothes, Benito? They had on priests' robes. Now, what could that mean?"

"Trouble. Wait, we can find out." Juarez caught a small boy by the shoulder. "Here, boy! What happened? What have those men done?"

The boy laughed. "Have you not heard, Señores? Oh, it was funny! That General Santa Anna—what will he think of next?"

"We are waiting," said Juarez. "Tell us what happened."

"It was like this," said the boy. "I went to church with my mama this morning. It is a very grand church. The rich people all go there. Today when

30

we got there, there were many men with priests' robes. They had the hoods pulled over their faces. They were very quiet. But then came the time to give the money. All those priests—they were not priests at all! They were Santa Anna's soldiers. They threw back their robes. They had guns!

"Then their leader made a speech. Right in church! With the guns pointing at the people! He said he would take the church money. He said he knew they would all be glad to give. He was going to use the money to make Guerrero president. But all those rich people had voted for Pedraza! That was the joke. Never have I laughed so much!"

"Very funny," said Juarez, never smiling. "Did they give their money, then?"

"Did they, Señor? Under those guns? The gold came rolling out. They put in watches and jewels—everything they had. The soldiers even took the poor box money. The soldiers are going to bring the money to Santa Anna now. Follow me if you want to see the show."

The boy ran off. Juarez and Miguel followed more slowly. Then Miguel spoke.

"Well, after all—. Have we not talked about it often enough? The rich take the last penny from the workers. Is this so bad? They have only taken back a little. The boy was right. It is funny."

"I don't think it's funny at all, Miguel. Robbing people is never funny. They brought shame to the church, too. They have broken the law."

Many other people were following the soldiers. They stopped a little behind the crowd. Juarez stepped up on a stone to see better. A line of soldiers came out of a building. They stood on the stone steps and rolled their drums. Then General Santa Anna himself stepped out.

The General raised his hand. Then his rich, full voice rang out on the sunny air. He began by telling the crowd what fine people they were. "I am only your servant," he said, smiling. "I am here to do what you want." Then he told them how the rich people were cheating them. The rich were bad. The poor were good.

Miguel soon stopped listening to this cheap talk. He looked carefully at the General. Santa Anna was now thirty-four. He was tall and slender. He looked fine in his beautiful uniform of red, blue, and gold. He wore the stars of a general. Nobody had ever made him a general, so he made himself one. "Well," said Miguel, "he can make it sound good and he looks good—even if he is a liar."

Santa Anna finished his speech. The crowd roared and clapped hands. They were all for him. Miguel laughed and looked at Juarez. The smile died.

Santa Anna was waving his gold-laced cap to the cheering people. He looked up and saw the young man on the stone. The General was surprised. There, dressed in a long black coat and black stovepipe hat, was the only man not cheering.

Juarez' mouth was closed tight. The black Indian eyes were staring straight ahead. The Indian face was like rock. Santa Anna frowned. Juarez just stared.

For a long minute they looked at each other. Then Miguel pulled at his friend's coat.

"Come on," he said. "The show is over. Let's eat."

"Yes," said Juarez. He followed Miguel back the way they had come. The crowd was growing bigger. They were calling for another speech.

"They will get it," said Miguel. "It will be the same speech again. He has only one speech. I must say, though, he does it well. He will put Guerrero in as president."

"Yes, I guess he will," said Juarez.

"Well, and why not? After all, we want Guerrero, don't we?"

"Even you!" said Juarez. "I know this man can get the people with him. But can't you see? What we want is important, yes. But there is something more important. That is HOW we get it. Santa Anna's way is by breaking the country's laws. I tell you this, Miguel—*that is not the right way!*"

Miguel was right. General Guerrero became president. He lasted a few months. Then his vice-president, Bustamente, "spoke" against him.

Whenever a Mexican leader wanted to start a revolution, he would "speak" against the one in office. That meant he would say the country was not being ruled right. The one who "spoke" usually had an army ready. To "speak" in this way was not law, of course. It was just a way of telling the people another war was starting.

Vice-President Bustamente turned out to be a conservative. He did not like Guerrero, so he "spoke" against him. He moved quickly—and promptly had President Guerrero shot dead. So now the conservatives were in power again. Santa Anna had called himself a liberal. He was not very popular in the capital.

Santa Anna did not like to be unpopular. So he went down to Tampico where some Spanish soldiers had landed. Spain had sent them to take Mexico back. Hundreds of the Spanish had died of yellow fever. Santa Anna beat the ones who were left.

So the "Hero of Tampico" called on the people to make him their president. Another election was held. Santa Anna was elected. Bustamente went out.

But Santa Anna had another surprise for his people. He had gone to his country home. Now, instead of coming to the capital, he stayed there. He wrote a long letter to the congress. He said his health was poor and his nerves torn from fighting. He must get back his strength. The new vice-president must run the country for a while. "You never know what the general will do next," the Mexicans told one another. They loved him for it.

He played this little game for three years. The vice-president, Dr. Farías, did the work. He was a liberal, and a good, able man. If Santa Anna had let him alone, the country would have gone ahead.

The big question in Mexico was about owning the land. The rich people owned the farms and the mines. Even the city land was owned by the rich or by the churches.

You did not have much of a chance if you were poor. If you worked as a farmer, you did not have your own farm. You could work for a rich man for very poor pay. If you did, you barely kept yourself alive. You could also be a sharecropper. That meant you farmed a rich man's piece of land. You had to pay so many bushels of the crop to him. If you had a bad year, that was just bad luck. If you made just enough to pay him, you got nothing.

Most of the Mexican Indians were bitterly poor. Yet the land was good. You could raise enough food so all could live fairly well. The liberals wanted to give the poor man a chance.

The 1824 constitution had been the first step. President Victoria tried to pass laws to help the poor workers. But the first congress did not draw up the laws very well. It was hard to make them work.

Dr. Farías tried to make these laws better. He had a liberal congress, and Santa Anna let him alone for a while. It seemed that at last Mexico would be a free republic.

It could have happened. The road seemed clear. But Santa Anna helped to spoil it. He was getting tired of his quiet life. He had been reading the life story of Napoleon. Napoleon had been a great soldier. Well, he, Santa Anna, was a great soldier, too.

About this time Dr. Farías made the army smaller. Santa Anna did not like that. He would have to put Farías in his place. He called for his horse. He called out his own army. Where could he fight another war? He rushed out and crushed a few rebels.

Now the conservatives began to plot again. Farías was working against them. They would have to get him out. Who could get him out? Why, the President himself. "You are Mexico's strong man," they said. "You must take over. Farías is dangerous. Save us."

Santa Anna was willing. He did not care if he was conservative or liberal. He just wanted to rule. Nobody knew yet how the new laws would work. The people were restless and uneasy. If the conservatives could work with Santa Anna, they were ready to do so. Santa Anna was ready, too.

He was willing to go over to their side. He was willing to wipe out the liberal laws to help the poor. He was willing to send the liberal congress back home. There was only one thing he wanted himself. He wanted to be the absolute dictator of Mexico.

So Santa Anna came back to the capital. He told the congress to leave. He said Dr. Farías was Mexico's enemy. He got rid of the new laws. The conservatives helped him. All the hard work of the liberals was lost. Mexico was again the rich man's country.

While all this was going on, Benito Juarez was trying to get started. He graduated from school. He took his bar examinations and passed. Benito Juarez was a lawyer at last. He hung out his sign and waited for work.

During his last school year Father Antonio had died. Josefa married and moved far away. Juarez still visited the Mazas. They now thought of him as a good family friend. Always he brought a toy or a piece of candy for little Margarita, José's sister.

Juarez was quiet and did not make friends easily. Almost his only friends were Miguel and the Mazas. The Maza house was full of fun and laughter. He was always happy when he left. But it was now different with Miguel. Always crippled, Miguel slowly became worse. He could no longer walk. He stayed in bed with his books. The end was not far for Miguel. He had grown more interested in politics and had high hopes for his friend Benito. When his father's friends came, he always talked about Juarez. "You liberals here need a man like Juarez," he would say. Every day he talked to Benito about politics.

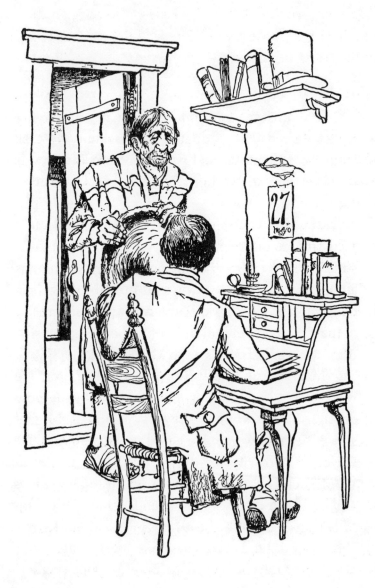

"Get into politics, Benito," he said. "Someday you will be a great man." He helped Benito get elected to the town council while they were still in college.

Benito Juarez had rented two rooms from a poor widow. One was his law office. He lived in the other. The office held an old desk, two chairs, and a shelf. On the shelf were the few law books he had been able to buy. Here sat Benito Juarez one October morning in 1834.

He looked up as a step sounded at the door. A very old Indian stood there.

"Can I help you, uncle?" asked Juarez.

The old Indian stood twisting his hat. "Please, sir," he said, "I have some trouble. I have no money to pay, though."

"That's all right," said Juarez. "Sit down. Well, tell me. Who are you and what is the matter?"

"Sir, my name is Juan. I am an Indian. I live in a village ten miles away. I tend a bean field, as my father did. Each year I must pay the owner a hundred measures of beans. What is left I get."

Juarez nodded. "You have a family, Juan? Your sons help you?"

The old man shook his head. "I had four sons, sir. But the army took them. Also, my wife is dead. I have only Pedro, an orphan boy. Pedro has been like a son to me. He is a good lad, sir, but he is simple. He cannot think much, but he works hard."

"Yes, Juan, I see. Has someone hurt Pedro?"

"Yes, sir!" The old man's eyes flashed. "I'll tell you about it. First, there was the bean crop. This year it was bad. I could get only thirty measures. It was not my fault, sir. It was the same for everybody. No rain fell."

"I see. You were not able to give the hundred measures?"

"That is right. When Don Manuel came for the beans, he was angry. He wanted a hundred measures. He would not take the fifty."

"Fifty? You said you had only thirty."

"I did. The other twenty I bought. I sold my goat and my blankets. I even sold the silver cross my wife had. It was not enough."

"And what did you do then?"

"What could I do? I gave Don Manuel the beans. He was very angry. He said he must take my mule, my little gray donkey. Ah, sir, Pedro loved it like a brother. We need the donkey, sir, for the work. But, sir, do not laugh! That donkey was Pedro's *friend*."

"Go on, Juan. Your landlord took the donkey?"

"Sir, this is hard to tell. Don Manuel got the donkey. He drove it out to the road. Poor Pedro, he could not understand. He put his arms around the

42

donkey's neck. He held on. Don Manuel hit him with his whip—many times. The boy rolled in the dust. Don Manuel drove the donkey away."

"I see. And you feel this is not fair?"

"I am only a poor Indian. I do not know the law. I know Don Manuel can take the donkey. I do not ask about that. It has always been so. But I have heard things have changed. I hear the white man has no right to hurt the Indians. I hear even the poor have some rights. Was Don Manuel right? Can he beat poor Pedro so his hip twists and he cannot walk again?"

"What's this?" said Juarez. "You did not tell me the boy was hurt. The law does not permit this. If this is true, Don Manuel goes to jail."

"But I have no money, sir."

"I told you that does not matter. Listen, Juan. I can not get the donkey back. You made the agreement with your landlord. It is not a fair agreement. Some time the law will stop such agreements. But it is still the law now."

"I know that, sir."

"You are right about Pedro. One man may not harm another man. We will bring Don Manuel to the judge. You and Pedro will tell your story. If the judge finds your story true, this Don Manuel will go to jail many, many months."

43

"Good!" cried the old man. "If Don Manuel goes to jail, it will not help Pedro's hip. But it will make many poor people glad. Don Manuel is a hard, cruel man. I will let Pedro see Don Manuel in the jail. I will—"

"Not so fast! What is his name, Juan?"

"Don Manuel Chávez, sir."

"Where does he live?"

"At the Blessed Mercy convent, señor."

Juarez laid down the pen. "I do not understand, Juan. He lives at the Blessed Mercy convent? Here in Oaxaca?"

"Oh, yes, sir. Did I not tell you? He is the head farmer for the sisters. The convent owns many farms. Don Manuel runs them."

"I see. Then the convent is your landlord. You should have told me this before, Juan."

"I am sorry, sir. I did not know it mattered. Don Manuel beat the boy."

"Yes—yes, that is true." At last he rose.

"Stay here, Juan. You will find bread and cheese in the next room. Lie upon my bed. Rest yourself. Wait for me."

Juarez put on the long black coat and the high black hat. He opened the door and went out.

It was evening when he got back. He hung up his hat and sat down. He looked sad.

44

"Well?" said the old man. "He is in jail now? Can I go look at him?"

"Juan, listen to me. Try to understand. First, some good news. I have seen Mother María at the convent. She is a kind lady. She was sorry to hear about Pedro. Tomorrow she will send for him. She will do all she can to make him well again."

"That is good, Señor. But how about Don Manuel? I want to see him in jail."

"I am sorry, Juan. There will be no jail for Don Manuel."

"But you said so! You said the law—"

"I will try to make it clear, Juan. There is such a law. But there is another law. This law says that soldiers and church men are judged by their own kind—other soldiers and church men. Don Manuel is no church man, but he works for the church. That means he has this right. We can do nothing to him."

"But—. I do not know much, sir. You are a lawyer. But if he can do this thing, it is not fair. I would go to jail. He does not. This does not seem right."

"It is not right, Juan," said Juarez. He shut his jaws tight. His black eyes gleamed. "I have done what I could. The sisters will nurse the boy back to health. They are kind, gentle women, Juan. They are not to blame."

"I know that, Señor."

"On earth only men work for the church, not angels. The day will come when these men must answer to the law, Juan."

"That will be a good day, sir. Will it come in our time, do you think?"

Benito Juarez looked at him, then past him. When he spoke, he said slowly:

"I cannot tell you when, Juan. But do not fear. It will come!"

CHAPTER 10. FIRST STEPS

In 1833 Benito Juarez went into the Oaxaca legislature. He came in with the liberals. He was still teaching and had only a little law work. Oaxaca the city was the capital of Oaxaca the state. Juarez did not have to leave home to go to meetings.

There were not many meetings. The constitution said the president should be elected by the state legislatures. So, when Santa Anna or Bustamente wanted to be elected, they put in their own friends. Then their friends would "elect" their hero.

Benito Juarez was the first to fight a vote for Santa Anna. He made a fiery speech against Santa Anna. "We must keep the constitution," he said.

"We have fought hard to get it. Now Santa Anna wants to throw it out. He wants to be a dictator."

Other liberals followed him. Santa Anna could never get the Oaxaca legislature to support him. The conservatives asked to hold off the vote until the next day. The liberals agreed.

Late that night a loud knocking awakened Juarez. He opened the door. A crowd of soldiers rushed in.

"You are under arrest!" cried one.

"Why?" asked Juarez calmly.

"You have been getting the Indians to rebel," said the soldier.

They hurried him to the city jail. Other liberals were already there. They could not get news to their friends.

They stayed in jail a few days, then were turned loose. When they got out, they found the vote had gone for Santa Anna. Other legislatures had voted the same way. And so Santa Anna became dictator of Mexico.

Santa Anna was ready for another war. He had it in his own country. The Texans were trying to get free of Mexico. They said Santa Anna had thrown out the constitution, so they were free. If there was no constitution, there were no Mexican states. They meant to set up their own republic. They had their own flag and their army was ready to fight.

This was a war Santa Anna liked. He was sure he could win. So he called his men and started for Texas. But there was little glory for him. He did butcher the hundred and sixty brave Texans at the Alamo. But the Texans paid him back at San Jacinto.

Texan Sam Houston captured Santa Anna himself. And so the "easy" war ended. It broke out again ten years later in the Mexican War with the United States.

When Santa Anna returned home, Bustamente had again taken over. The General was not popular because of the war. It was no time to try to win the people again. He slipped quietly to his country home to wait his chance.

Benito Juarez kept building up his law work. Every day he became better known. His first cases had been poor men who could pay nothing. But he won those cases. Soon the richer people began to use him. He knew the law and he was honest. In 1842 Juarez was made a judge.

Now, for the first time, he made money. The judges got good pay. He gave up his two little rooms and bought a house. Benito Juarez looked ahead. Should a judge not have a wife? Benito Juarez thought he should.

Margarita Maza, José's sister, was now a beautiful
girl of seventeen. Like her mother, she had red hair
and blue eyes. She was the only girl in a family of
boys. But even that did not spoil her. She always
showed good, common sense. Being a girl in Mexico,
she did not go to school with the boys. She learned
to sew, to paint, to play a little music. Everybody
expected Margarita to marry a rich young man.

On a spring evening in 1843 the Mazas were sitting around after dinner. Señor Maza and his wife
were sitting at a table. The younger boys were out.
José and Margarita were playing chess in a corner.

"Listen!" cried José. "There is that step outside
again. That is not somebody just passing by. He
comes and he goes. That is another one of your boy
friends, Margarita. Last night it was Carlos. The
night before it was the García boy. Always one of
your boy friends must march before the house.
That's what we get for having a beautiful sister."

"Oh, José, don't be silly!" said Margarita. But
Margarita, too, was listening to the steps. Up and
down before the house they went.

"When are you going to peep out, Margarita?" laughed José. "You must wonder who it is. Do you hope it is Carlos?"

"Oh, no! I can't stand that Carlos. He wears a new velvet coat every week. Always he must look in the mirror at himself. He's like a girl. I don't like him."

"He's the best looking lad in Oaxaca. He's rich, too. Oh, well. How about young García? Captain García, I should say. How about a dashing young soldier?"

"I could never marry Antonio García," she said. "His father beats the Indians on their farm. They are a hard, cruel family. I want nothing to do with them."

"Say, you are hard to please. What are you waiting for? A prince from over the sea?"

"I'm in no hurry to get married."

"That's right," said Señora Maza. "You are only seventeen. You still have a year or two. Have no fear. We shall find a good husband for you."

Outside the footsteps kept marching.

"Whoever it is doesn't give up," said Señora Maza. "Have you peeped out yet, Margarita?"

"Not yet, Mama."

"Well, do so," said her mother. "Who is it?"

The girl rose and went to the window. She moved the heavy curtains aside. She looked out into the

street. She stood there, not moving. They all saw she was blushing.

"Well? Well?" said Señor Maza. "Who is it? Get me my cane. I will rap three times on the floor. That will bring him in."

The girl ran to her father. She threw her arms around his neck.

"No! No! Papa, do not do it yet! It is too soon."

"Aha!" laughed Señor Maza. "You want to keep him waiting, do you? You have been home from school six weeks now. Every night someone is playing bear outside. Why wait if you have made up your mind?"

"Which one was it, Margarita?" asked José. "And why have you changed your mind? Was it Carlos or Antonio?"

She laid her head on her father's shoulder. "It was neither one, brother," she said.

"Neither?" cried her father. "I have nothing against them. Who was it, then? Tell us, little one."

"I was surprised, too," the girl said. She spoke shyly. "It was—It was Don Benito."

"Benito! OUR Benito?" shouted Señor Maza. "He wants to marry you? But, my dear, he is older than your oldest brother. José, has he said anything to you about this?"

"Not a word, father."

"He must be twenty years older than you. Yes, he is now thirty-seven. He is not a rich man, my dear."

"Also, he is an Indian," said Señora Maza. "I should have Indian grandchildren. What would my people say?"

"Mama, please!" Margarita's face was red. "Nothing is settled. There is no hurry. This is the first time he has been outside. Maybe he will not come again. We must wait and see."

It seems strange now—this "playing bear." But all the Mexicans did it. Benito still came to visit the Mazas on Sunday nights. He said very little to Margarita. No one said anything about playing bear.

But every night now, the footsteps passed the window. The old custom had come from Spain. There the young man would sing or play music to the girl. The custom had changed in the Mexican cities. Now he just marched outside the house. It might go on for weeks or even months. Then the family might call him in. If they did not like him, he marched until he gave up.

Benito Juarez marched many weeks, playing bear. Margarita had to change her parents' minds. Benito Juarez was no handsome hero. He always wore a judge's clothes. That meant black trousers and a long black coat. He wore a stiff collar and a tall, shiny black hat. He was short, with strong, heavy shoulders. He had high Indian cheekbones and a brown Indian skin. But he had a high forehead, steady, honest eyes, a gentle mouth, and a rocky chin. Margarita made no mistake when she chose him over more handsome men.

Margarita waited until she was sure her parents would agree. Then she waited a little longer. But at last the night came. Benito Juarez, walking outside, heard a welcome sound. From inside the house came three raps of Papa's cane.

He went to the house then and knocked. A servant opened the door. The whole family was waiting. They talked about the weather. They brought out wine and cake. Then Juarez went home.

The nights of playing bear were over. Now Juarez had to call on the family a while. Then he asked to speak to Señor Maza alone. The two went into the dining room. It was a room Benito remembered well. Here Señor Maza had agreed to let him be his kitchen boy.

They talked a long time. At last it was over. The two men came back. Señor Maza had his arm around Benito's shoulder. He smiled and took Benito over to Señora Maza. She, too, was smiling now.

He bowed low. "Madam," he said, "I want you to meet your new son-in-law!"

Benito Juarez and Margarita were married August 1, 1843. Then followed a few quiet years. The first child, Manuela, was born. She looked just as her mother had. The Juarez family was a happy one.

But Mexico was having her troubles. From March, 1843, to December, 1846, Mexico had nine presidents. The liberals and conservatives were still fighting. Worst of all, war was near.

Santa Anna was now president, now out. He still thought he could easily beat the Texans. The Texans, though, had the United States behind them now. Santa Anna seemed to think he could beat anybody. "Let the Yankees come," he cried. "I, Santa Anna, will chase them back home."

In 1845 the Texans joined the United States. American General Zachary Taylor camped on the Rio Grande. The Mexicans had never agreed that the Texans were free. So now they felt the Americans were coming into Mexico. The Americans said Texas had been free and was now one of the United States. On April 25, 1846, the Mexican army crossed the Rio Grande. They met a few Americans. They attacked and killed some. President Polk said blood had been spilled on American land. He said the war was started. You know the story of the war from your histories.

In 1847 the people elected Benito Juarez governor of Oaxaca. Juarez was no soldier. He had to raise men and money for the army. He did a good job. He needed money for other reasons, too. Benito Juarez remembered how hard it was for poor Mexicans to go to school.

He had not forgotten his own hard life. He could not forget the sneers because he was an Indian. Always he had dreamed of bringing schools to his Indian people. Now, as governor, he was able to do something about it.

He started with his own college. He sent young men out to the little villages far away to set up schools. There were not enough books. Juarez ordered them by the thousand from Europe. He paid high prices to Mexican printers to print books.

All this took money. The only way Juarez could get it was by taxes. Nobody likes to pay taxes. But the people soon saw that he collected them fairly. They saw he was spending the money honestly. He would not keep workers he did not need. The tax money went for schools, not to the politicians. When Juarez left in 1852, there was 50,000 pesos, or

Mexican dollars, in the state treasury. Usually the state owed money.

The people elected Juarez again as governor. In his second term Señor Maza died. He left a house to his daughter. The house was in the little town called Etla, a few miles from Oaxaca.

The governor's house was cold and damp. There were four babies now, so Margarita wanted to move to Etla. The family spent more and more time there.

When Juarez' second term was over, they all stayed at Etla. His years as governor had been hard ones. He decided to take his first vacation. His law work was waiting, but he had a little money saved.

José Maza often came to the Etla house to visit. He always brought the latest news. The news was never good. Santa Anna and the conservatives were in power again. The Mexicans had forgotten that he had lost the war with Texas. The "Mexican Napoleon" was having his last hours of glory.

"Say, Benito," said José, "let's go down to your old village, Gualetao. The Indians down there are proud of you."

Benito smiled. "Yes," he said. "My people have been kind to me. I hear Apolonio, the horse trader's son, is mayor now. They say my Uncle Bernardino speaks very highly of me now."

"I hear it's a beautiful little valley. You know, I

still like to paint. I could paint some pictures and you could see your old friends."

"All right," said Juarez. "You go to Oaxaca first. Buy us some strong mules. Pick up some presents for my old neighbors. Get Uncle Bernardino a bottle of wine. We will take a little vacation, but then I must get back to work."

CHAPTER 13. CAPTURED

José bought the mules in Oaxaca. On a bright spring morning the two friends started out. The family was there to say good-bye. They gathered at the gate and waved. The trip was to last only a week. The family did not know they would not see their father again for two years.

The road was only a stony path, twisting and winding. But the mules were used to the country. They went along steadily. About noon they came to a shady spot.

"Here is a good spot," said José. "Let's eat our lunch."

"All right," said Juarez. He looked around with a smile. "I have been here before, you know. This is where I stopped on my way to Oaxaca when I was a boy. I remember bathing my feet here. They were bleeding. My lunch was fern leaves."

"You ATE fern leaves?"

"There was nothing else. I'm glad we have a better lunch today."

They got out the lunch. As they started to eat, they heard the sound of horses and men's voices. The men were singing. Both knew the tune. It was *Muchos Calzones*—"Many Pants." It was the marching song of Santa Anna's soldiers.

The men came riding around the corner. There were about thirty soldiers. They wore the uniforms of Santa Anna's men.

The leader shouted when he saw José and Benito. The others let out a yell. They jumped off their horses and grabbed their guns. Before the two could get up, thirty guns were pointing their way. The captain came forward.

"Benito Juarez and José Maza?" he asked.

"Yes," said Juarez calmly. "What do you want?"

"You'll soon see," said the captain. "Men! Tie them up."

The soldiers quickly obeyed. José fought and pulled away, but Juarez stood quietly. He kept his eyes on the captain's face.

"Are we under arrest?" he asked. "What have we done to be arrested?"

"Don't you know?" sneered the captain. "Do I have to tell you?"

"You do. My friend and I have broken no law."

"Are you not on the way to Gualetao? We know you are."

"Is that wrong?" cried José. "Why shouldn't we?"

"You shut up!" said the captain. "We're not after you. We want Juarez. He is a traitor. Do you admit it, Juarez?"

"Admit what? What have I done?"

"We know why you're going to Gualetao. You want to stir up the Indians against Santa Anna. You are going to meet other rebels there. What do you say now?"

"It is not true, captain. I know this is not your own idea. Show me your warrant for my arrest. I'll be glad to go back to Oaxaca. Just take me to court—"

"Oh, you won't tell, eh?" cried the captain. "All right. I can waste no more time. Tie them on their mules, men. We have a long ride."

"The warrant, captain," said Juarez. "The law says you must show me your warrant."

"The law!" laughed the captain. "You know law, don't you, Juarez? Well, let's see how much it will help you. Put him on the mule, men. Here—!"

The captain stepped back. Juarez had heaved his

broad shoulders. Two Mexican soldiers went flying. Juarez stepped up to the captain.

He did not raise his voice. Calmly he said, "Yes, captain, I know the law. I hope you do, too. Who gives you the right to arrest me?"

"General Santa Anna, president of Mexico!" shouted the captain. "Is that enough?"

"It is not. When we reach Oaxaca—"

The captain sneered. "When we reach Oaxaca, Juarez, you can do as you please."

They soon found out what he meant. They started north, not south to Oaxaca. They stopped at a town for three days. No one spoke to the prisoners. A soldier brought them bread and water.

Later they stopped at other towns. Always Juarez and José were treated badly. Juarez wished to send word to his family. The soldiers would not let him write a letter.

"This is not right," Juarez said to José. "This is against the law. All prisoners may write letters. These men have nothing against us. No judge will send us to jail."

"Yes," said José, "you're right. But I don't see any judges around, do you?"

It was past midnight. The prisoners lay on their beds. José turned and twisted. Juarez slept. Then voices outside awakened them. The soldiers came in, carrying torches. They cleared the way for a young man who now came in.

"Prisoners!" called the guard. "Here is José Santa Anna, the great president's son."

He moved to one side. The president's son was very young—not more than eighteen. He was fat. He had hardly any chin. His neck was hidden in a four-inch collar. The coat was a beautiful, flaming red, covered with gold lace. His chest was filled with shining medals. His boots shone like glass. A short blue cape with a fur collar hung over his shoulder. His sword was covered with jewels. He held a silver helmet in his hand.

Benito Juarez had not changed clothes for two weeks. He had even slept in them. He had not washed his face or combed his hair. Young Santa Anna looked at him and sneered. But Juarez was not ashamed. He looked the young man calmly in the eye for a long moment.

"I am glad you have come, sir," he said. "I think somebody has made a mistake."

"Mistake?" said young Santa Anna. "I don't think so, Juarez. My father wanted you arrested. My father does not make mistakes. But I don't want to talk to you. Get ready to leave."

"Gladly. I want to see the president—"

"I don't think you will, Juarez. The president is a busy man. He doesn't want to see traitors."

"I am not—!" Juarez stopped. "Then I want to see a judge."

"Oh, you want, do you? Everybody knows you are my father's enemy. You are Mexico's enemy. Do you remember that you would not let my father through Oaxaca? Or did you forget? We were fighting the Americans, too. Maybe you have forgotten. My father has not."

"Ah, yes," said Juarez. "I remember very well. The Americans were in Mexico City. General Santa Anna had run away. He was a general no longer. He wanted to get through Oaxaca. I would not let him through. If that was wrong, then I am wrong. I did that. I'm glad I did."

"Aha! You admit it!" cried young Santa Anna. "All right. You shall see what Mexico does with traitors."

"Sir," said Juarez, "my friend Maza here has

64

nothing to do with this. Will you let him go? I want him to tell my family where I am."

Santa Anna turned to José. "Go!" he said. "Get out. But be careful what you say. You had better not say anything against my father."

They let José loose and gave him his mule. Juarez told him what to tell his family. "Say that I am in no danger," he said. José promised. He got on his mule and galloped away.

Before morning Juarez was moving again. This time they used a carriage. A soldier holding a gun sat beside him. Twice a day a new guard came in. The guards brought Juarez bread and water. Sometimes they let him walk a little. But each time they blindfolded him.

He had no idea where he was going. The soldiers never spoke. Day and night they rattled on. Juarez lost count of the days. He sat quietly, sleeping when he could.

The trip finally ended at Vera Cruz, on the coast. They threw Juarez into jail here. He stayed here a few days, until young Santa Anna came. The soldiers brought Juarez to him.

"Juarez," said he, "you are a lucky man. My father will show you mercy. You are a traitor. You should die. But my father says he will not kill you. Get out. Get out of Mexico. Don't ever come back. There is a British ship here. She is going to Havana. You sail on this ship. If you ever come back, you are a dead man."

Juarez' face was like a rock. "What about my family?" he said.

"We won't bother them, Juarez. My father is a great man. He does not fight women and children."

They let him go then. They even let him wash. But all his bags were gone. His money was gone. He had to wear the same shirt he had worn for four weeks. He had not a penny in his pockets.

CHAPTER 15. IN NEW ORLEANS

The street looked like an alley. The houses were old and very dirty. José Maza stopped before the third house from the corner. He set down his heavy bag. José wrinkled up his nose. Pigs were rolling in the mud under the front steps.

José took a letter from his pocket. He looked again at the address. No, there was no mistake. This must be the place. He climbed the steps and knocked on the door. Then suddenly the door flew open.

The woman was big, fat, and dirty. "Well, what do you want?" she snapped. "I'm busy."

"I would like to see one of your roomers, please," said José. "I would like to see Benito Juarez."

"Not here," she said. "He works." She was about to close the door.

"Wait," called José. "I need a room, too. Can you give me a room?"

"A room? Why, I have none just now. But I can put a bed in your friend's room. There are others, but there will be room for one more."

"Let me see the room, please."

The house smelled of cabbage. He followed her up the stairs. She went down a dark, dirty hall. She knocked on a door. A weak voice inside called, "Come in." She threw open the door.

The room was small. On the floor lay three mattresses. A man lay on one. He raised himself as the door opened. He was thin and sick. His eyes were bright with fever.

"General Montenegro!" cried José. "Benito wrote you were here. I did not know you were sick."

"Just a little fever." The sick man held out his hand. "I'm glad to see you, Señor Maza. Benito does not know you were coming. No bad news, I hope? His wife and children are well? We have had no letters for many weeks."

"My sister and the children are well. But much has happened—"

67

"Well," broke in the woman, "you have seen the room. I can put a bed in for you. You'll have to pay me now for a week. That will be three dollars."

"If you haven't got much money, you'd better stay," said Montenegro.

"All right," said Maza.

Montenegro was an old liberal general. He had fought Santa Anna long and bitterly. Santa Anna had forced him out a year before. Juarez had met him in Havana. Together they had come to New Orleans.

"I wish I had some money," said José. "I'd like to get you and Benito out of here. They took all my money. But what has happened to Benito? He says so little when he writes. He wrote my sister he was getting along well. We thought he was teaching."

"He did not want her to worry," said Montenegro. "There are many of us here. We are all poor. Ocampo—you remember him?—he lives here, too."

"Ocampo? Why, he was a very rich man."

"Santa Anna took everything away from him. You know what he's doing now? He makes cooking pots. He sells them in the streets."

"I can't believe it. What does Benito do?"

"Benito Juarez, lawyer, member of congress, governor of his state, now is—a cigar maker. He sits all day in a dirty cellar. He rolls small, cheap cigars."

"But Benito is a learned man! Are you joking?"

"No, I'm not. Do you know what I do? I sell bananas from door to door. I'm not very good at it, either. I'm glad my father put me in the army."

It was dark when Juarez and Ocampo came home. Ocampo brought the supper—bread and sausages.

"José!" cried Benito. "This is a surprise. Has Margarita sent you? Is she sick? Tell me the worst."

"Margarita is well, Benito. She and the girls send you their love. But that is not why I am here. I have been talking too much—about the great Santa Anna. They told me to get out—while I had a chance."

"Could you not have brought Margarita and the children? I don't like to have them alone."

"Benito, I do have some bad news. They have taken everything you owned. They left only the house at Etla. I hate to tell you this, Benito. You have not a cent left."

"Never mind that," said Juarez. "My wife—how is she to live? You should have brought her, José!"

"Cheer up, friend!" said José. "It's not so bad. They left her the house. Well, what do you think she has done? She got a little money and opened a shop in the front room. She sells all sorts of things. The people flock in. Everybody in town loves Margarita. They even buy what they don't need. That's

69

what they think of you. You need not fear. She and the children are doing fine."

José told them what Santa Anna was doing. He now had a "court." He made his friends dukes and counts. Everybody wore bright new uniforms.

Benito Juarez did not say much. He had always fought for a free Mexico. He wanted the poor to have a chance. He knew all too well how much the Mexicans loved a show. Well, Santa Anna knew how to give it to them. And the country had no money. Santa Anna's men were stealing what they could. The money spent on uniforms could have fed starving people.

José laughed as he told about the silly things Santa Anna was doing. But Benito Juarez did not even smile. He did not think it was funny at all.

CHAPTER 16. A LITTLE HOPE

As José said, he had little money. After the first night he set out to find a job. That was not easy. Mexicans were not much liked in New Orleans. Americans had not yet forgotten about the war. They still thought the Mexicans were enemies.

There were other Mexicans in New Orleans. Some

of them were famous liberals. Santa Anna had forced them all out of Mexico. Those who did not get out were in jail. Some were shot.

These men did what work they could to live. Every night they met and made plans. Someday Mexico should again be free.

One of these men was General Comonfort. He had escaped with some of his own money. He wanted to share it. But Juarez had a better plan.

"Let's save this money," he said. "Let's try to get more. If we are ever going to win out, we shall need money. We'll have to buy guns and pay soldiers."

"But how can we get more? We have a hard time living now," said the others.

"Comonfort is a good man. He can talk," said Benito. "Let's have him talk to some rich Americans. Some of them may give or lend us money. He will have to dress well and live like a gentleman. There are rich men in New York and Boston and Philadelphia. Let's send him to talk to them."

And so General Comonfort set out. Early in 1854 he came back to New Orleans. He had five thousand dollars in his pocket. But he had something even better. A Connecticut gun factory owner had agreed to send them the guns they needed. He would ship them where they wanted in Mexico. They would pay when they could.

71

There was more good news in a letter from Mexico. The poor people were getting tired of starving. A revolution was starting out on the Pacific coast. There General Juan Alvarez, an Indian soldier, was leader. Alvarez had fought for Mexico against the Americans. His band of Indians had helped Santa Anna. After the war he could not get along with Santa Anna. He had gone back to his farm. He still ran his part of the country, though. Now over seventy, he was going on the warpath again.

Already he had captured Acapulco, the sea port. This was good news. Here was a place for Comonfort to land those guns. He left for Mexico to tell Alvarez about them. They sent word to the gun factory and looked for a ship. The Panama Canal had not been built yet. To get to the Pacific coast meant a trip around Cape Horn.

The ragged, homeless men went down to see Comonfort off. The five thousand dollars was safe in a belt around his waist. They were all hungry and their feet were bare. But not one of them thought of touching a cent of that gold. It was to make Mexico a free country again.

Comonfort reached Acapulco in February. He got in touch with old General Alvarez at once. A few other leaders joined them. The general's son came.

On March 11, 1854, these men met at Comonfort's home in Ayutla. There they wrote their Declaration of Independence. It called for Santa Anna to be overthrown. A congress was to write a constitution. The declaration is known in Mexican history as the Plan of Ayutla.

CHAPTER 17. THE LAST OF SANTA ANNA

In September, 1855, a dirty little steamer stopped at Acapulco. The ship's cook got off. He was Benito Juarez. He had not had enough money for the trip around Cape Horn. He paid his way on a ship headed for Panamá. Then he walked to the Pacific side. There he found a ship captain who let him work his way to Acapulco.

"Where is General Alvarez?" he asked.

They told him he was many miles from the coast. But Diego Alvarez, the general's son, was in town. He was waiting for a ship load of guns. Juarez went to find him.

Young Diego was eating. His servant came in.

"There is somebody here to see you, sir," he said.

"Who is it?" young Alvarez asked.

"I don't know. He is dressed in rags. Looks like a beggar, but acts like a gentleman."

"Well, send him in."

Juarez did look like a beggar. His clothes had been old and worn when he left New Orleans. He had worked on the greasy steamer for weeks.

"You wanted to see me?" said young Alvarez.

"Yes, sir. My name is Juarez. I know you are fighting for liberty. I have come to help."

"Oh! Well, that is good. We need men. But just now we have more men than guns. You have no gun?"

"No, Señor. I have no gun."

"Well—I don't know. By any chance, can you write a little?"

"Yes, Señor. I can write."

"Good. Can you do a little arithmetic? My father needs a man to keep track of things. Would that be too hard for you?"

"No, sir. I could do that."

"Fine! That is settled, then. I will give you a note to my father."

He called his servant. The servant found a pair of pants for Juarez. Diego gave him an old shirt. Juarez would have to walk all night to get to the camp. There were no blankets. So young Alvarez took the blanket off his own bed. That was Juarez' *serape*—the blanket which is overcoat and bed to the Mexican.

He walked all night. The next afternoon he found old Alvarez in his tent. He gave his name and the note from Diego. Juarez and Alvarez had met before. But that was long ago. The old general's eyes were getting weak. He thought Juarez was a stranger. Juarez did not tell him who he was.

General Alvarez was glad to have a new clerk.

"I have one now," he said. "He is a young student named Porfirio Díaz. Oh, but he is smart. Two more years and he would have been a lawyer! Think of it—a real lawyer! A man with such brains should not be a clerk. And he is a soldier! Every day he asks me to let him fight. Now that you are here, he can fight. Are you sure you can write?"

"Yes, general, I can write."

Comonfort had gone to Mexico City. Santa Anna's government was already slipping. Comonfort was talking to the soldiers. They were tired of the dictator.

Margarita Juarez knew her husband had left New Orleans. She wrote to Comonfort, asking for him. Comonfort knew nothing. He hoped he had gone to Alvarez. So he wrote to Juarez, in care of Alvarez.

Young Alvarez gave out the mail when it came.

The first letter was addressed to Lawyer Benito Juarez. He looked at Juarez, the new clerk.

"Oh, Juarez," he called. "Come here a minute. There's a letter here with your name. I think some-one is playing a joke."

Juarez took the letter. "It is for me, colonel," he said.

"For you? But—oh, it is a joke, then. See, they call you a lawyer. Why should they do that?"

"Why, I am a lawyer," said Juarez.

"You? A lawyer? Wait, let me see that name again. Benito Juarez. You mean THAT Benito Juarez? The judge? The governor of Oaxaca? Are you that Juarez?"

"Yes, colonel. I am that Juarez."

"But—I had no idea. It is a common name. But my father should have known you. Think of it! You, the governor of Oaxaca—and I gave you Juan's second best pants! Why did you not tell us who you were?"

"But why? I am not very important."

Alvarez looked at him in surprise. Benito Juarez really meant it. He had asked to fight for freedom. He did not think he was too good for anything.

Young Alvarez told his father. The old man quickly found other work for Juarez. He became Alvarez' secretary. Juarez wrote all Alvarez' letters.

Other news came in the mail. Santa Anna had left

in August. Some said he was going to fight rebels at Vera Cruz. His wife had gone there before him. She had taken many things with her. Later they turned out to be oil paintings which belonged to the government. Now other news came. Santa Anna had gone aboard a ship going to Havana.

A week later they found the news was true. Mexico City was for the Ayutla Plan. The people had torn down Santa Anna's statue and dragged it to the city dump. When Santa Anna heard this, he ran. He took everything he could and fled.

CHAPTER 18. THE JUAREZ LAW

But Mexico's troubles were not over. The government had no money. Business and farming had almost stopped. Many young men had done nothing but fight. They did not know how to make a living. Santa Anna had been the government. Santa Anna was gone, so there was no government.

The liberals decided they needed a new constitution. They made Alvarez president until they could write it. You cannot write constitutions overnight. They called the men together. It took them two years to finish their work.

So Alvarez ruled the country. He was much more at home in the saddle than as president. He began well enough. First he named his cabinet. Ocampo was in it. Comonfort was named Minister of War. Benito Juarez took care of the courts and the schools. This is what Juarez always wanted to do. He lost no time writing the Juarez Law. He brought it to Alvarez to sign.

Juarez had never forgotten Juan, the old Indian. Don Manuel had never been punished for hurting Pedro. Because he worked for the church, he was above the law. Juarez had promised that someday it would be different. Old Juan was dead, but the day had come.

The Juarez Law took away the favors of the soldiers and the church. Church men and soldiers were to have the same rights as others. Alvarez talked it over with the cabinet. Ocampo was for the new law. Comonfort was against it. He thought it was a bad time to stir up the conservatives. He wanted to change the laws a little at a time.

Juarez did not want to go slowly. It was high time they had such a law, he said. The liberals were in power. The argument grew bitter. Even these good friends could not agree.

Poor General Alvarez listened to all of them. The whole thing just gave him a headache, he said. He wanted to wait. Let the law lie on his desk a while. He would make up his mind later.

After a few days he did sign it. As Comonfort had said, the conservatives stormed angrily. They still owned the newspapers. They wrote angrily against the new law. The priests preached sermons against it. "Resign!" they cried to Alvarez. "Get out before the people throw you out."

But Alvarez' army was strong and they were with him. The conservatives could not force him out. "Stand firm," said Juarez. "Let them talk all they want. The trouble will soon die down. Once they see the laws are good, they will say no more."

The old general was brave enough. He was not afraid, but he did not like the trouble. He was from the country. He was an Indian. Mexico City seemed an unfriendly place. He wanted to go back to his farm. There he would not have to listen to this talk about laws.

So he went to the congress and resigned. He thought Comonfort could handle the angry conservatives best. He asked the congress to name him president. He was afraid Juarez would get into trouble. So he asked that Juarez be sent to Oaxaca as governor again.

Everybody was satisfied. Comonfort and Juarez just could not get along. Comonfort wanted to go slowly. He was glad to have Juarez away in Oaxaca. Juarez wanted to go where he could do the most good. He was glad to go back to Oaxaca.

There was enough work there. Everything Juarez had built up, Santa Anna had torn down. Weeds grew on the fine new roads. The schools were closed. Juarez' own college had been empty for years.

He opened the college first. Then he did everything all over again. It was a busy time, but a happy one, too. Margarita and the girls had joined him in Mexico City. They were all glad to go back to Etla. A new baby was born there—the first Juarez boy. They called him Benito. Later came the twin girls, María and Josefa.

Juarez took over as governor in 1856. The Mexican congress was still trying to write a constitution. Juarez now got out a new constitution for Oaxaca. It was a good one. Before 1856 ended, the people voted Juarez in again as governor.

The Mexicans finally finished their constitution in 1857. It was much like the United States Constitution. The Mexicans kept it until 1917.

One difference was in the supreme court. The Mexicans elected their supreme court judges. The president of the supreme court was vice-president of the country.

The first election under the new constitution came

81

in November, 1857. Comonfort was made president.

Benito Juarez was elected president of the supreme court and vice-president. Again the little family left Etla to go to Mexico City.

CHAPTER 19. TROUBLE ONCE MORE

The Juarez Law was not the only one which angered the conservatives. There was another one called the Lerdo Law. The Lerdo Law said that land could be owned only by a person—not by the big companies called corporations. Corporations had to sell their land at fair prices. The great Mexican church orders were corporations.

The Juarez Law and the Lerdo Law were in the new constitution. The conservatives said these laws meant the death of religion. They always said the bitter war that followed was a religious war. Their cry was "For God and Holy Church."

But religion had nothing to do with the war. Those who wrote the new constitution were almost all church members. Only one did not belong. The others did not think of leaving the church. The Lerdo Law let all churches keep church property.

The liberals believed in the church. They did not

think the church should be a big land owner. They thought it was wrong for a poor Mexican to work his life away on a church farm. They wanted him to have a chance to own his own land.

The conservatives thought these ideas were foolish. They said the liberals were fighting the church. They tried to get the church to fight the liberals.

Mexican life was always close to the church. The government did not even keep birth records. The church kept those when children were baptized. You could get married only in the church. You were buried in holy ground. Mexicans could hardly live without the church.

Juarez' new laws gave these rights to the government. The government was now to keep birth records. The government would keep marriage and death records. The conservatives would not agree to that.

All new government men had to swear to uphold the constitution. Conservatives said they would put them out of the church if they did. Some did. Other church leaders took the new laws.

Comonfort thought he could keep the conservatives satisfied. No man could have done that and put in the laws. Comonfort was only a man. He could not do it, either.

Juarez was little help to him. Juarez could see no

sense in trying to satisfy everybody. Either your enemy is right or he is wrong, said he. If he is right, do not be his enemy. If he is wrong, change his mind. If you can not change his mind, fight him.

But the conservatives were ready to fight, too. They said only blood could wipe out the new constitution. They wanted to put Iturbide's son on the throne. A young soldier, Miguel Miramón, was their leader. He soon forgot about Iturbide, though. He got more interested in himself.

All over the country trouble was starting. A few miles from Mexico City a man named Zuloaga was raising an army. Zuloaga broke Comonfort's hopes of peace. This Zuloaga had owned a big gambling house. Santa Anna's men often gambled there. Nobody had money to gamble, so Zuloaga decided to become a soldier. He got the conservatives to help him. He soon had a strong army. They ate better and had better guns than the government army.

In 1857 Zuloaga said the new constitution would never work. He called for Comonfort to throw it out. Comonfort, he said, should rule as a dictator. He marched his army to Mexico City. The congress had to leave. Juarez said he was a traitor. Zuloaga had Juarez arrested.

Nobody knows whether Comonfort planned this. Some people think he did. Others think it was

Zuloaga's idea. Comonfort said the constitution was dead. He was willing to rule as dictator. He was sick of war. He hoped to keep everybody happy.

But seventy men of congress met outside of Mexico City. When they heard what Comonfort had said, they moved fast. They said he had broken his oath as president. That meant he was no longer president. The congress said Benito Juarez was now president of Mexico.

By law the congress was right. Even Comonfort must have known that. He had Juarez brought from jail to his palace. He begged Juarez to resign. Juarez would not do it.

The liberals were not sleeping, though. News came that Santos Degollado, a liberal, was forming a new army. He meant to fight for the constitution. Zuloaga was ready to fight him. But Comonfort did not know what he wanted to do. One day he talked to the conservatives. The next day he talked to the liberals. He tried to please everybody.

Zuloaga got tired of him quickly. He told Comonfort to get out of Mexico and stay out. Comonfort went. Just before he left, Comonfort took the guard off Juarez. Juarez quickly joined the congress. He was just in time. Zuloaga called himself president and sent his army after him. The Three Years' War, bitterest of all Mexican civil wars, had begun.

The Three Years' War is also called the War of the Reform. It came just before our own War Between the States. The two wars were much alike. The slave question split our North and South. The question of poor men's rights split Mexico. Lincoln felt he had to fight to keep our country together. Juarez felt the same way about Mexico. Lincoln was a man of peace and not of war. Juarez was such a man. He felt the constitution must be saved. If only war could save it, Juarez was willing to fight.

Juarez took the president's oath and named his cabinet. News came that Zuloaga was coming. The new government left for the Pacific coast.

Degollado joined them there. He had raised a big army. They decided to bring their two armies together. Degollado would lead them both.

His army had hard times in those early days. The conservatives still had almost all the money. They were able to pay soldiers better and to buy better guns. The government had nothing. They were not able to do much until 1859. Then the United States said that Juarez was president of Mexico as far as we knew. That helped the liberals get what they needed.

The liberals decided their best chance to get money was at Vera Cruz. Vera Cruz was the big seaport. There the government could collect money on incoming goods. Also, they could stop shipment of guns to Zuloaga.

So Juarez and the cabinet started for Vera Cruz. But all of Mexico was between them and Vera Cruz. Zuloaga's army was close behind. The only way to go was by sea. Juarez and a few others sailed first to Panamá. They had to walk across the land to Colón. Here they got a boat to Havana. From Havana they went to New Orleans, then to Vera Cruz. The trip took almost three weeks.

The Mexicans in Vera Cruz were glad to see them. The government there had already voted that Juarez was the president. They meant to help him fight Zuloaga. They had sent no money in to Mexico City, but had held it for Juarez. The liberals needed the money badly and were glad to get it.

President Juarez made a speech at Vera Cruz. He told the people they were facing a long, hard war. He told them why they were fighting and why he would never give up.

The first year of the war went badly for the liberals. They were able to hold Vera Cruz. One by one the members of congress got there. Juarez was able to set up his whole government. The liberals held some places on the Pacific coast, too. But the Zuloaga government held most of Mexico. The liberals were not strong enough to attack Mexico City. They had to hold what they had.

Zuloaga was not so eager to fight after he became "president." He had some good generals, though.

One was Miguel Miramón. Miramón was a twenty-six-year-old Frenchman. He was so handsome people said the girls fainted when they first saw him. But Miramón was a good soldier. He had fought the Americans as a boy of fifteen. Zuloaga picked him because the rich conservatives liked him. Zuloaga had made his way by gambling. He needed help from the rich, old families.

At first they got along well. Zuloaga and Miramón never did become close friends, though. Zuloaga liked General Márquez better. Márquez, like Zuloaga, had been a Santa Anna man. He was cruel and out to help himself. He later proved to be both a coward and a thief.

The third Zuloaga general was Mejía. This man was an Indian like Juarez. He believed that white men were better than Indians. He thought the Indians should work for the whites. When Juarez tried to help the Indians, Mejía thought he was foolish. He was honest and fought for what he believed.

Zuloaga did not stay long. Miramón was too popular. Even the army liked Miramón better. He was a daring, reckless fighter. In December, 1858, the army held their own election. They elected Miramón president and told Zuloaga he was through.

Miramón was gone just then. When he got back, he found himself "president." Miramón would not take the job. He asked that Zuloaga stay as their leader. But Zuloaga saw how the wind was blowing. He backed out. Finally Miramón agreed.

There were two presidents in Mexico. France, England, and Spain agreed that Miramón was the real president. They sent their men to deal with him. These men liked him. A Frenchman said he was just like a king.

That pleased the conservatives. They thought a king was just what Mexico needed. Why not Miramón? He himself believed in kings. He would not turn down a crown.

If Miramón could have won the Three Years' War, he would have been king. But there was another president. Down in Vera Cruz was a grim, tough Indian. He was not young and handsome. He never had been handsome. He still signed his papers "Benito Juarez, president of Mexico." The people had elected him and he was going to stay.

Many friends thought it was no use. They begged him to quit. Miramón, they said, was a good man. The country would not do badly if he were president. If Juarez would give up, they could have peace. What chance did the liberals have? Why not end it now?

Juarez always listened. He heard all the arguments. Then he gave his answer. It was a simple one. HE had been elected. Miramón had not been elected. If the people wanted Miramón, let them hold a free election. That is what the constitution said must be done. Until they did, he was going to do his duty. He was president of Mexico. He had to uphold the constitution. Miramón was a rebel against that constitution. A president swore to fight the rebels. That is what he, Juarez, was doing.

That was his stand. Nobody could shake him. Right was right and wrong was wrong. He was going to do the right as he saw it. Benito Juarez had always been like that.

CHAPTER 22. VICTORY

Miramón won all the big battles. Degollado never won a battle. But when he lost, he always kept his army and was ready to fight again. The liberals finally won because they would not give up.

The war was a cruel one. General Márquez became known as the "Tiger." He shot all prisoners in cold blood. Even Miramón did not trust Márquez. Once he arrested him for stealing. But as the war went on, Miramón needed more money. Márquez could always get it. In 1860 he broke into British government offices and stole $620,000. The British howled about it so loud that Juarez had to pay it back later.

Late in 1859 the United States recognized the Juarez government. That gave Juarez a chance to get guns. His government needed them badly. They were still short of money. They did what Miramón was doing—borrowed it. Nobody had any idea how they would pay it back. Nobody worried much about it then. There was a war on. Wars cost money.

By 1860 the United States' guns were pouring into Vera Cruz. The conservatives had no port and were running low. The rich men were getting tired of helping an army which did not win.

The liberals were fighting better, also. Degollado was still losing, but was never beaten. Another general, Escobedo, was winning. Escobedo had been a mule driver. He had never been inside a school. He said if a man could handle mules, he could handle men. He seemed to be right. Juarez made him a colonel and then a general.

In 1860 the liberals gave Miramón a good beating. General Ortega won this first big victory. Degollado gave up his command to Ortega. Ortega now got the army together and set out for Mexico City. Márquez tried to stop him, but took another beating.

Miramón was now back in Mexico City. He led his army out against Ortega. Ortega cut his army to pieces. Miramón barely got away. He slipped to the coast. There a French boat picked him up and took him to Europe.

Ortega camped his army outside Mexico City. He sent word to Juarez to come. "The city is ours when we want it," he wrote. He could see the white flag flying over the city. The people began to come out to tell him what good liberals they had always been.

Ortega hoped they could make a grand parade into the city. He made all the plans. He even went in at night to pick the streets for the parade. The tailors came to make new uniforms. Finally the plans were all made.

But Juarez seemed in no hurry. Days passed. No word came from Vera Cruz. When the letter did come, Juarez said he wanted no nonsense. He was coming, but he wanted no parade. Ortega, he said, might well get to work.

Two weeks later a black carriage rolled into the city. There were no crowds. Few turned to look. There were no bands, no flags, no marching soldiers. A quiet Indian in a long black coat and a stovepipe hat got out. The president had come to town.

CHAPTER 23. A SON FOR JUAREZ

It was late afternoon in July, 1861. The president's last caller had gone. Juarez sat at his desk. A pile of papers lay before him. It was growing dark. His secretary came in carrying an oil lamp.

"Good, Pedro. I was going to send for you. You have finished the letters? Then get home, boy. You must be hungry."

"I'm not hungry, sir. But will you not come now? Señora Juarez asked me to supper. She wants us to come together."

Juarez looked at the papers. "No, no," he said. "I cannot leave yet. Go on, Pedro. Do not wait for me. I shall be late again."

"Yes, sir." The young man waited a moment. "Can I do something to help, sir?"

"Help?" Juarez gave a short laugh. "I don't think so, Pedro. Look at this!" He held up a paper. "This is what we owe the British. Our soldiers broke into their stores. We took one of their trains. They ask us to pay back $620,000 which Márquez stole."

"But that was robbery! Surely the British do not ask us to pay for our enemies?"

"It's not so simple, Pedro. We are the Mexican government. We had to protect them. We were not able to. We must make good. I wish the others were as easy to deal with as the British."

"You mean the Spanish and the French, sir? I added the numbers."

Juarez nodded. "The French are asking twelve million dollars. They have bills going back forty years. Miramón borrowed money to fight us. We have to pay that back. If we don't, no country will trust us. We borrowed money from the United Sates to fight the war. We must pay."

"Yes, sir. But how?"

"Oh, we shall pay. We shall pay. But now we have nothing. We are going to begin at home. For two years we will build back the country. Then we can make money again. When we can, we will pay what we owe. Well, you had better go on, Pedro."

"I wish you would come too, sir. You are tired."

"Maybe you are right. I am tired." He took his black hat. "Come, lad. Call the driver."

The old black carriage stood outside. It was geting dark as the two got in. Juarez worked in the president's palace. He lived in his own house. Other presidents had lived in the palace. But Juarez lived a simple life.

Pedro Santacilia, the young secretary, cleared his throat.

"Sir—" he began.

"Yes, Pedro?"

"Sir—" he tried again. He was very young. His voice cracked a little. Then he got it out. "Sir, I don't know how to say this. Sir, I want to marry your daughter."

Juarez frowned. "What nonsense is this? My daughters are children. You know that."

Pedro swallowed hard. "Manuela, sir. She is not a child. She is seventeen."

It seemed only yesterday that Manuela had been a baby. The next two had been girls. Then came the first boy, Benito. He had another son now, too. But José, the new baby, was weak and sick.

"Well, Pedro—" Juarez said at last with a smile.

"Yes, sir?"

Juarez laughed. "I was older than you when I married Señora Juarez. But I remember how nervous I was. Do you love my daughter?"

"I do, sir. I do."

"Then there is no more to say. Pedro, I guess I have a new son."

CHAPTER 24. PEACE TROUBLES

The Three Years' War ended in January, 1861. In March the people elected Juarez to another four-year term. Although the war ended, fighting still went on. Márquez was still free.

After the war Ocampo, Juarez' friend, went back to his farm. Márquez caught him on the way and killed him. Juarez made up his mind Márquez would pay for the murder. First he sent Degollado after the "Tiger." Márquez caught Degollado and a hundred fifty men. Márquez took Degollado prisoner, then shot him dead.

Next Juarez sent General Valle with more men. He fell into Márquez' trap. Márquez killed him, too.

The third man to go was Porfirio Díaz. Díaz was

a general now, and a good one. He caught Márquez and gave his soldiers a beating. But Márquez himself got away. He took a few men and slipped into the mountains.

In July, 1861, Juarez said he would not pay Mexico's bills for two years. In the same week came the first big battle of the American War Between the States. The war kept the United States busy. She could not worry much about Mexico.

England, Spain, and France did not want to wait for their money. They wanted it right away. They thought Mexico was full of gold and silver. They thought they could come in and cut the gold like cheese.

They did not know how hard it was to mine in Mexico. What Mexico had was silver, rather than gold. It was spread all over the country. It lay in the mountains far away. The silver had to be hauled over many miles of mountain roads. Nobody was in the mines. The men had all been fighting. The mines were flooded. They had made cannon out of the machinery. Buildings had been burned.

Juarez knew all this. He meant to get the silver out. He thought he could get the country going in two years. Then he hoped to pay these countries. But he was not going to get two years.

This is where the War Between the States comes

in. The Monroe Doctrine was then thirty-eight years old. In it President Monroe had said America was for Americans. That meant the European countries should stay out. Up to this time, no European country had tried to move in. But now the United States had its own war. The United States could not fight a European country. If any country wanted to come in, now was the time to try it.

CHAPTER 25. FRANCE HAS A BILL

England, Spain, and France talked it over. They decided they were going to get paid. If the Mexicans would not pay up, they were going to make them. In December, 1862, Spanish soldiers landed at Vera Cruz. Later British and French warships landed.

Juarez sent General Doblado to meet them. They held a meeting on a Spanish warship. Doblado came with the figures. He made it clear that Mexico had no money to pay. He brought a letter from President Juarez. The letter promised that Mexico would pay after two years.

The English saw Juarez meant it. They agreed to wait two years. The Spaniard, General Prim, agreed that Spain would wait, too. But not the French.

The Frenchman, Saligny, had orders from Napoleon III. Napoleon III was Napoleon Bonaparte's nephew. He said Mexico owed France twelve million dollars. The Mexicans were going to pay—now.

While the argument went on, a new French army landed. With the army was a Mexican named Almonte. Almonte had been living in Paris. He was an old friend of Santa Anna. Almonte said he had come to save Mexico from Juarez. Napoleon III would help him, he said. The army was there to prove it.

The English and the Spanish saw the way the wind was blowing. They knew Napoleon III wanted to win new lands. Canada, he thought, really belonged to France. The Louisiana Purchase had been an American trick. If he could get Mexico, he might get more.

The Spaniard and the Englishman saw the French did not want the money. They were going to use the money as an excuse. Once in Mexico, they planned to stay there. The excuse would look good if England and Spain helped.

They wanted nothing to do with this plot. They called Doblado and told him Juarez' plan was fine. Early in April the British and Spanish ships left.

But the French stayed. There were six thousand now, and more were coming. Almonte wanted to start for Mexico City. On the way he wanted to take Puebla. He had heard guns were stored there.

The "guns" were old ones in a museum. They were the guns the British had taken from the French at Waterloo. Mexico's first president had bought them.

The Mexicans in Puebla got the old guns out. They loaded them and calmly awaited Almonte. Zaragoza, a good Juarez general, led them. When the French came up the hill, the Mexicans cut them down. But Napoleon III was not ready to give up. He sent a new army under General Forey. This time there were 30,000 men.

They took Vera Cruz first, cutting off the money to Juarez. Then they planned to take Puebla. Juarez rushed help there. Ortega and Díaz went to help.

The French began attacking the city on March 16, 1863. The city held out for two months. The starving people ate every animal inside the walls. When the last bullet was gone, General Ortega had to give up. Ortega and Díaz both got away.

The enemy were near Mexico City now. Juarez and his few men had to leave. The best of their army had been at Puebla. The French got into Mexico City without trouble.

Now the conservatives came out of hiding. They were glad Juarez was gone. They welcomed the

French happily. General Forey wrote Napoleon III that the Mexicans wanted France to save them.

Now Forey went around getting the conservatives together. He called a quiet little meeting. He had a letter ready for them to sign. The letter asked Napoleon to send them a king. The king was already picked out. He was Maximilian Hapsburg, younger brother of the emperor of Austria. Napoleon III had picked him, Forey told the conservatives.

The conservatives went wild with joy. They had always wanted a king. Now they would have one. They all wrote their names. The letter did not go to Austria. It went to Paris. Napoleon III read it. He liked it. He sent for some Mexicans living in Paris. They took the letter on to Austria.

Maximilian was a gentle, pink-cheeked, blue-eyed young man. He wrote poems and played the flute. He collected butterflies. Max was a kind, well-meaning, simple man. He saw good in everybody. More than anything, he wanted to make people happy.

His wife was different. She was Charlotte, sister of Belgium's king. She did not love everybody. She hated her brother-in-law, the Austrian ruler. She hated Napoleon's wife. She wanted her Max to get ahead.

Charlotte was eager to go to Mexico. Her Max would be a real king. She would be a queen. She would be as good as anybody else. She began telling her Max to go.

Max was not sure. He did have a chance to make a whole country happy. But did the Mexicans really want him? He wanted to be sure. News came that the Mexicans had voted to have him. Of course French General Forey had taken care of that. Only conservatives had voted.

Charlotte had looked at the map, too. What she saw surprised her. Mexico was three times as big as France! Why should Max be just a king? He should be called Emperor of Mexico. She told Max he could make her happy by going.

"I wish to make you happy, dear," he said. "We will go. Also, I can make all those poor Mexicans happy—my people."

"OUR people, darling," said Charlotte sharply.

In the summer of 1864 President Juarez was at Monterrey. His cabinet and his family were with him. Only thirty men were left in his army. They had no shoes and few guns.

Maximilian and Charlotte were on the way. Maximilian had already borrowed a hundred million dollars for Mexico. Max did not worry about money. He was writing a book. The book was for his Mexican people. It was a rule book telling them how to

102

behave in court. Max said the people could read the book and not be ashamed of themselves. "And so," he said, "they will all be very happy."

CHAPTER 26. ANOTHER PARTING

'Finish eating, children. Leave the room. I want to talk to your mother."

"Yes, papa. Good night, papa. Good night, mama."

The Juarez children rose and left the room. Manuela, now married a year, was the oldest. The twins were seven. Benito was the oldest of the three boys.

Señora Juarez spoke to Manuela. "Will you sit with little José? He has slept an hour now. I think the fever is over. If he wakes up, call me."

"Yes, mama. Shall I take the baby?"

"No. I will hold him."

The older girl got the children to the bedrooms. She went to sit with José. José was barely alive.

"What is it, Benito?" asked Señora Juarez. She looked down at the baby on her lap. Little Antonio had been born in Monterrey two months before. He, too, was sick.

Juarez put his hand on her shoulder. "I have asked much of you. Now I must ask something again."

She touched his hand. "Whatever you say, Benito."

"Listen, then. Margarita, I must send you away. You and the little ones. You must go to the United States until this war is over."

"Benito, no! Not that. Do not ask that. I don't mind the danger. That means nothing. I don't care as long as we are together. Don't send me away."

"You make it hard, Margarita. I have thought about it for weeks. The French are pouring soldiers into Mexico. Maximilian sits in Mexico City. We are being pushed into Texas. Díaz says we cannot hold Monterrey. We must move soon again."

"That's all right. Where you can go, the children and I can go. Our place is by your side."

"Margarita, listen. You must think of the children. José is very sick. He needs a good doctor."

"José is better. He will grow strong."

"José has never been strong. There are good doctors in the United States. And little Antonio! He is always crying. He is sick, too."

"I know. I know."

"Márquez has joined the French. Do you remember Ocampo? Do you want him to find our children?"

He watched her face get white. He hated to say what he did. But Juarez always told the truth.

She rocked the baby until he was quiet. Then she laid him in his bed. She came back to his side.

"When must we go?" she said quietly.

"Tomorrow, my dear. There is no time to lose. Pedro Santacilia will go along. He speaks English well. He will look after you."

"Tomorrow! I must pack the children's clothes." She moved away, then stumbled. He caught her in his arms. She began to cry bitterly. He patted her head. At last she lifted her face.

"When shall we see you again, Benito?"

He looked past her, out into the street. "Don't be afraid, dear," he said. "We shall meet again when Mexico is free."

CHAPTER 27. MAXIMILIAN

The old black carriage rattled off to the nearest seaport. Little Benito and the twins rode a donkey. Pedro rode his horse. Juarez did not dare go along. His few soldiers might leave. He walked to the end of the town and watched until they were gone.

Maximilian had been in Mexico about three months. Nobody worked. Here and there armies were fighting. The French waited for Maximilian to collect their money. The conservatives waited for him to get rid of the liberal laws. The rich people wanted their land back.

Maximilian had to do other things first. He picked the place for the new Fine Arts Palace. He laid out the streets running to it. He rebuilt an old Spanish castle. Maximilian and Charlotte had given thirty luncheons, eleven dinners, six balls, and twenty receptions.

And Max had to have his picture painted. He brought over a French artist to do that. One picture was not enough. He had five done.

Charlotte had her own ideas. She had brought some German women to wait on her. Now she sent them home. She picked the wives of the Mexican leaders to wait on her. She wore Mexican dresses, but had them made in Paris. She changed her name to Carlota.

But the French money was going fast. No money was coming in. The French army had not beaten all the Mexicans. Still, they were happy in Mexico City. The fighting was far away.

The good times did not last. Carlota was sharp with the Mexican ladies. She sent them home to learn their manners. They did not like that. Their husbands began to listen to them.

Then Maximilian really got himself into trouble.

His first cabinet, he said, would not all be conservatives. There were liberals among his people, too. He must be fair to all. His conservative friends looked at each other with open mouths. He asked them to name a few liberals.

They tried to tell him that only the conservatives wanted a king. The liberals did not want a king. The liberals had a president. The liberals did not want him. They did not want the French in Mexico.

Maximilian just smiled. "But you forget, gentlemen," he said. "They voted to have me come. They wanted ME as their ruler. I rule not only the conservatives. I rule all Mexico—by the people's will."

Again they looked at one another. They all knew how the "vote" had gone for Maximilian. But they could hardly tell him.

"Oh, yes," said Maximilian. "They tell me this Juarez is not bad—for an Indian. I shall write to him and ask him to be in the cabinet. It will show my good feeling. That's what we need here in Mexico. Yes, we must be one big, happy family."

He was surprised when he got Juarez' answer.

"A man may take another man's rights," he wrote. "He can take his goods. He can kill those who fight for their country. But one thing he cannot do. He cannot keep men from judging him. Some day history will judge you."

Juarez' blackest year was 1864. He was pushed back to the Texas border. He made his last stand across the river from El Paso. The city is now called Juarez. He was almost alone there. Díaz had gone to raise an army in Oaxaca.

Díaz did get the army together. But he lost his first battle with the Frenchman, Marshal Bazaine. Díaz was captured, but he got away. He then joined old General Alvarez. Alvarez got men and guns to help him.

By spring, 1865, things began to change. In April, Lee gave up to Grant to end the War Between the States. While the war was going on, the United States could do nothing. But President Lincoln had never recognized Maximilian's rule. He had welcomed Juarez' man. Secretary of State Seward had always been Mexico's friend. Now Seward began to prove his friendship.

They sent an American army to the Rio Grande. The soldiers did not cross the river. But they were there, at Juarez' back. Napoleon III soon heard what the Americans thought of Maximilian. The United

States would be friendly only if the French soldiers got out.

Napoleon thought he would have a war if he did not get them out. Maybe Seward was bluffing. The United States had just fought a long war. She was not ready to fight France. But if it was a bluff, it worked. Napoleon wrote Bazaine to try once more to crush Juarez. After that he should come home.

Napoleon had other reasons. A man named Bismarck was leader of Prussia. He had his eye on France. It looked like war to Napoleon. If war came, Bazaine and his thirty thousand men would be needed. Napoleon had his own troubles. He did not worry much about Max.

Marshal Bazaine talked matters over with Maximilian. The two got out the famous "Black Decree." The Black Decree said that everybody fighting against Maximilian would be shot. That meant no prisoners would be taken.

But the battles were going against Max now. The Black Decree could not stop that. The Americans began dumping great piles of guns on their side of the Rio Grande. They put no guards over them at night. In the morning the guns would be gone. General Sherman never said a word to Juarez' General Escobedo. Americans began to enlist in the Mexican army, too. Soon Bazaine's Mexicans began

110

to drift in. They were getting tired of fighting their own people.

Marshall Bazaine thought Maximilian would go back with him. But Carlota did not give up so easily. She said she herself would go to France. She would ask Napoleon III not to take his soldiers away. If he would not listen, she would ask her brother, the Belgian king, for help. She would save them all, she told Max. Max must not worry any more.

She sailed from Vera Cruz in July, 1866. She never saw Max or Mexico again. She died in Belgium in 1927 after sixty years of being hopelessly insane.

Bazaine was now getting ready to leave. "Come on," he said to Max. "You had better resign and get out of here."

Max did write out his resignation. Day after day he carried it around in his pocket. One day he wanted to leave. The next day he would want to wait a while longer.

Bazaine made his last call. The French ships were waiting at Vera Cruz. It was time to get out.

Max told him to go on if he was in such a hurry. The French army had been a mistake anyway. A Mexican ruler should depend on Mexican soldiers. "Why," he said, "I will lead them myself. Yes, that's what I will do. I will fight myself. The people who love me will fight for me."

When Bazaine heard that, he wasted no more time. He got out. The next day the French soldiers marched out. Max did not even say good-bye. They had been his friends. They had fought bravely and well. Many had been killed. But Max was too busy that day. He was holding a meeting with his new generals. The three were Márquez, Miramón, and Mejía.

Only Márquez had been friendly with Max. Miramón had wanted to help, but Max had turned him down. Now he was glad to have him back. Mejía came, too. The three and Max made their plans.

Some European soldiers had stayed. They, with some Mexicans, were to fight under Miramón. Márquez and Mejía were to raise Indian armies. Max himself would be commander-in-chief.

Miramón and Mejía went about two hundred miles northwest. There they built up their army. They soon had nine thousand men. Max thought it was time for him to start fighting. He joined the two.

Juarez' General Escobedo went after them. Márquez was back in Puebla. General Díaz had him well cornered there. Díaz was getting better with every battle. Escobedo pounded Maximilian's army to pieces. On May 15, 1867, Max gave up at the Hill of Bells. Miramón and Mejía gave up with him.

An army court tried the three. They were charged

with fighting against their own lawful government. Seven Mexican officers made up the court. Maximilian had two well-known Mexican lawyers. Frederick Hall, an American lawyer, helped, also. The trial lasted a month. It was an open trial. The newspapers told what happened each day. The court said all three were guilty. The sentence—death.

When the trial started, everybody knew what the end would be. Nobody has ever said the trial was not fair. Max was guilty. He had taken power when he had no right to take it. He had never even lived in Mexico. He fought a war against the government of Mexico. He had signed the Black Decree. He had seen prisoners shot.

His friends now began to beg for his life. They failed. With Juarez, the question was simple. The court was trying Maximilian. The law said if he was guilty he must die. The court was fair and open. If the court said he was not guilty, he would go free. Nobody needed to beg for his life.

But the law, said Juarez, was the law. It must be obeyed. What if Maximilian was a prince? What difference did that make? Long ago Juarez had made a promise to a poor old Indian. "The day will come," he had said to old Juan, "when no man shall be above the law."

On June 19, 1867, at the Hill of Bells, three men

114

faced the firing squad. Maximilian Hapsburg, the foolish prince, died bravely. General Mejía and General Miramón died with him.

CHAPTER 29. MARGARITA COMES HOME

The flags were flying on a July day in 1867 at Vera Cruz. Most of them were Mexican flags. But here and there was a United States flag, too. The two countries were very friendly now. The United States had helped a lot in getting rid of the French. The Americans had shown great honor to Juarez' wife in Washington.

Señora Juarez had lived quietly in New York for two years. She visited Washington on her way home. President Johnson had asked her to stay at the White House. He had ordered an American war ship to take her back to Mexico. Today she would come. The president had asked that the day be a holiday.

Bright blankets hung from the houses. Flowers were everywhere. Little boys ran through the streets carrying banners. Big letters on the banners read "Welcome, Mama!"

The streets had been filling since morning. The sun rose high and the people still waited. There were mothers with babies in their arms. Old men were leaning on their canes. Indians walked about, sucking on sugar cane. These were the poor people. The rich people had rented their houses for the day, bringing their own chairs. They sat on the porches.

People down the street began to cheer. From the mayor's house came an empty carriage. Four white horses were pulling it. The people had brought Carlota's golden carriage for their president's wife. Even the harness was gilded.

At last came the boom of a cannon. Every head turned. A deep cheer went up. The American gunboat *Wilderness* was steaming in. The doors of the customs house opened. President Juarez in his black coat and hat came down the steps. He walked up the gangplank. The American sailors stood at attention. The ship's band broke into the Mexican National Hymn. The ship's guns roared.

Pedro Santacilia ran forward. Juarez shook his hand.

"This way, sir," said Pedro. "She asked to see you alone."

She stood among her children. She was now thin and gray haired. Her arms, which had always held a baby, were empty now. Juarez held her in his arms.

"Well," he said at last, "here you all are."

"Here we are—those who are left!" cried Margarita. Her voice broke. She buried her head on his shoulder. "Oh, Benito, Benito—I have not brought you back your sons."

"Hush, my dear. I know. I know."

Little José had died in New York. So had the baby Antonio. Pedro had written Juarez. The Americans had been very kind. The best doctors in New York had done their best. Many Americans had written, saying how sorry they were.

Juarez patted Margarita's shoulder. Somebody pulled at his coat.

"I'm here, papa," whispered young Benito. "Look, see how big I am."

"And look at us, papa," cried the girls.

The children were all excited and tried to talk at once. Margarita dried her eyes.

They stepped ashore. A narrow path was clear through the crowd. A line of carriages waited. Carlota's golden coach was first. The Vera Cruz mayor was waiting there. The mayor ran forward.

"Sir, will you and Señora Juarez sit in the first coach? We will put the children in others."

Juarez shook his head. "Señor Mayor," he said, "I know you mean to honor me. I am glad you want to honor my wife. We both thank you. But she is a simple Mexican woman. We do not want to ride like kings. Send that golden carriage away. We do not want to use it."

They pulled the golden coach away. Margarita stepped into the same old black one. Juarez sat down beside her. Benito sat on his father's knee.

They had just started when the crowd stopped them. Eager hands pulled the harness loose. They led the horses away. Then, up the long hill to the mayor's house the people pulled the coach. It was a way to show the president their love for him.

CHAPTER 30. VIVA MEXICO!

People say that after the French had gone, Juarez gave Mexico her first real government. Before then the laws worked in some places, but not in others. Always there had been a party fighting the government.

Now the government ran smoothly. The French had done one thing for Mexico. They had brought the country together. The country now went liberal. The conservatives had learned their lesson. Many of them came over to the liberal side. Those who did not were not popular. Most people thought of Maximilian when they thought of the conservatives.

They had had enough of that. Juarez and the liberals stood for a free Mexico.

Even the religious question seemed to be settled. The church had lost her power as a big landowner, but she did not lose the people. People were no longer angry about the Juarez Law or the Lerdo Law.

There was much work to do. Mexico was millions of dollars in debt. But Juarez had never been afraid of work. The people elected him again in 1867, and once more in 1871.

Something was wrong on the evening of July 18, 1872. Every day the Juarez girls walked down to get their father from work. They walked together. The president was sixty-six years old now.

The girls were doing their best to take their mother's place. She had died a few months before. She had had four happy years after she came back. She had seen her second girl married. She had held her first grandchild. Now she was gone. Almost overnight Juarez turned into an old man.

On this July evening, no girls came to the president's door. No young Benito came to walk with his father. "The president—has anyone seen the president? He is always with his children now. Has something happened?" The people who saw him walk home every day did not see him this evening.

Whispers flew from one to the other. Someone said the president had not worked today. Who could believe that? The president worked every day. The people began to turn down the street where he lived. Before the house stood a carriage. Everybody knew it. It was the carriage of Juarez' doctor.

A man came through the door of the president's house. He stopped when he saw the crowd gathering. The man was pale. It was José Maza, Margarita's brother, who lived in the president's house. An old man spoke to him.

"Tell us, Señor Maza. It is not—the president?"

"We know it cannot be," cried another. "The president is never sick. He never spent a day in bed. Tell us, Señor. Who is sick?"

José tried to smile. He could not. "It is the president," he said. "The doctor has no hope. Excuse me, please. I am going to get the vice-president."

A groan came from the people. They stood and waited. Twenty minutes later Maza came back with Lerdo, the vice-president. The two went in and shut the door.

Word spread through the city. All through the night the people came to stand bareheaded in the street. Twice carriages came to the door. In the first one were Pedro and Manuela. Manuela was crying.

121

A servant came out, going to the drug store. The people asked eager questions.

"A heart attack," she said. "The master is awake, but has great pain. He has asked for Señora's picture. He says the room is growing dark. And four big lamps are burning! The children and the good friends are there. It cannot be long. Señor Lerdo is writing down his last wishes."

She went on down the street, crying.

It was growing light when the door opened again. Maza, Lerdo, and the doctor came out. Tears were on Lerdo's cheeks. José was crying. The old doctor held up his hand.

"People," he said, "Benito Juarez, president of Mexico, is dead. Here is your president now." He laid his hand on Lerdo's shoulder. He was the younger brother of the Lerdo who wrote the law.

Lerdo had run against Juarez in the last election. He had not always agreed with Juarez. But now he spoke for all Mexicans.

"People," he said, "you do not want a speech from me now. I say only one thing to you. Benito Juarez was Mexico. While Mexico lives, Juarez can never die. He would have me say—'Viva Mexico!'"